ARABIC ASTRONOMY ...GY
ISATION CALCULUS ... ...RY
MMERCIAL CORRESPONDENCE ... ...TO

KU-194-496

G CRICKET DRAWING DRESSMAKING DUTCH DUTTON
ELECTRICITY IN THE HOUSE ELOCUTIONIST EMBROIDERY
NGLISH RENASCENCE TO THE ROMANTIC REVIVAL ROMANTIC
RYDAY FRENCH TO EXPRESS YOURSELF FISHING TO FLY
BOOK GARDENING GAS IN THE HOUSE GEOGRAPHY OF
ARY GERMAN GRAMMAR GERMAN PHRASE BOOK GOLF
OOD FARM ACCOUNTING GOOD FARM CROPS GOOD FARMING
ARMING GOOD GRASSLAND GOOD AND HEALTHY ANIMALS
GOOD POULTRY KEEPING GOOD SHEEP FARMING GOOD SOIL
HINDUSTANI HISTORY: ABRAHAM LINCOLN ALEXANDER THE
CONSTANTINE COOK CRANMER ERASMUS GLADSTONE AND
ON PERICLES PETER THE GREAT PUSHKIN RALEIGH RICHELIEU
OW ... EMENT
N ... ETTER
GIN ... ANICS
RN ... ORING
OSO ... HYSICS
MBI ... UBLIC
CKO ... USSIAN
TS N ... AND
WA ... METRY

····AND HE WILL BE YET WISER *Proverbs 9.9*

AND PURPOSE SOCCER SPANISH SPE
SWEDISH TEACHING THINKING TRIG
BRI H RAILWAYS FOR BOYS CAMPING FOR BOYS AND GIRLS
R GIRLS MODELMAKING FOR BOYS NEEDLEWORK FOR GIRLS
S AND GIRLS SAILING AND SMALL BOATS FOR BOYS AND GIRLS
K FOR BOYS ADVERTISING & PUBLICITY ALGEBRA AMATEUR
BIOLOGY BOOK-KEEPING BRICKWORK BRINGING UP
Y CHEMISTRY CHESS CHINESE COMMERCIAL ARITHMETIC
VELLING TO COMPOSE MUSIC CONSTRUCTIONAL DETAILS
DUTCH DUTTON SPEEDWORDS ECONOMIC GEOGRAPHY
EMBROIDERY ENGLISH GRAMMAR LITERARY APPRECIATION
ROMANTIC REVIVAL VICTORIAN AGE CONTEMPORARY
SHING TO FLY FREELANCE WRITING FRENCH FRENCH
E GEOGRAPHY OF LIVING THINGS GEOLOGY GEOMETRY
BOOK GOLF GOOD CONTROL OF INSECT PESTS GOOD
M CROPS GOOD FARMING GOOD FARMING BY MACHINE
GOOD AND HEALTHY ANIMALS GOOD MARKET GARDENING
OOD SHEEP FARMING GOOD SOIL GOOD ENGLISH GREEK
Y: ABRAHAM LINCOLN ALEXANDER THE GREAT BOLIVAR BOTHA
NMER ERASMUS GLADSTONE AND LIBERALISM HENRY V JOAN OF
PUSHKIN RALEIGH RICHELIEU ROBESPIERRE THOMAS JEFFERSON
ME NURSING HORSE MANAGEMENT HOUSEHOLD DOCTOR
NALISM LATIN LAWN TENNIS LETTER WRITER MALAY
ENTS WORKSHOP PRACTICE MECHANICS MECHANICAL
MORE GERMAN MOTHERCRAFT MOTORING MOTOR CYCLING
Y PHYSICAL GEOGRAPHY PHYSICS PHYSIOLOGY PITMAN'S
E PSYCHOLOGY PUBLIC ADMINISTRATION PUBLIC SPEAKING

Kirstin M Paton -

THE TEACH YOURSELF BOOKS
EDITED BY LEONARD CUTTS

GERMAN

Uniform with this volume
and in the same
series

Teach Yourself Afrikaans
Teach Yourself Arabic
Teach Yourself Chinese
Teach Yourself Dutch
Teach Yourself English Grammar
Teach Yourself Esperanto
Teach Yourself Finnish
Teach Yourself French
Teach Yourself Everyday French
Teach Yourself French Phrase Book
Teach Yourself More German
Teach Yourself German Phrase Book
Teach Yourself German Grammar
Teach Yourself Greek
Teach Yourself Hebrew
Teach Yourself Italian
Teach Yourself Italian Phrase Book
Teach Yourself Japanese
Teach Yourself Latin
Teach Yourself Malay
Teach Yourself Norwegian
Teach Yourself Polish
Teach Yourself Portuguese
Teach Yourself Russian
Teach Yourself Russian Phrase Book
Teach Yourself Spanish
Teach Yourself Spanish Phrase Book
Teach Yourself Everyday Spanish
Teach Yourself Swahili
Teach Yourself Swedish
Teach Yourself Turkish
Teach Yourself Urdu

TEACH YOURSELF

GERMAN

A BOOK OF SELF-INSTRUCTION IN GERMAN
BASED ON THE WORK BY SIR JOHN ADAMS,
M.A., LL.D., COMPLETELY REVISED AND
ENLARGED BY SYDNEY W. WELLS, B.A. AND
FURTHER REVISED BY E. S. JENKINS, B.A.

THE ENGLISH UNIVERSITIES PRESS LTD
102 NEWGATE STREET
LONDON, E.C.1

First printed in this form 1938
New Impression 1958

Printed in Great Britain for the English Universities Press, Limited
by Richard Clay and Company, Ltd., Bungay Suffolk

PREFACE

WE have travelled a long way on the road since the Englishman, tall and skinny, with sandy hair and protruding teeth, was made the butt of ridicule on the Continental stage, and his attempts to speak a foreign tongue were found either irritating or excruciatingly funny.

We have progressed much, too, in our approach to the study of foreign languages. We are not so content to signal and gesticulate for our food in a foreign restaurant, and our eyes no longer flash with indignation at these " damned foreigners " who cannot speak the King's English. It used to be quite common, too, for a well-educated man to turn out a creditable essay in French or German on the fossil iguanodon, yet be distressingly inarticulate when called upon to order a second-class railway ticket or a dinner. Amusing mistakes, of course, will always be made. There is the Scot, for instance, who translated : " J'aime la langue française " by : " I love the tall French girl," or the German who said in great indignation to the waiter in a London restaurant : " I am here since ten minutes—when do I become a sausage ! " He had forgotten that bekommen in English is *to get*, while the English *become* is in German werden.

Most of the difficulties of forty years ago were due to an undue importance given to grammar and Classical subject-matter : the teaching did not help the practical man who wanted to travel. It is claimed for this book that the interests of such people are studied throughout. The classified vocabularies should prove very helpful, and it is hoped that the student will find that the bugbear of German declensions loses some of its terrors as presented here.

Anyone who follows this course conscientiously should be able to read, write and speak the German language with some measure of success. His accuracy and his fluency will depend not only on his native ability but also on his determination to keep at it regularly: a short time every day over a long period is much better than gigantic efforts every now and then.

INTRODUCTION

To know a language properly implies the power of using it freely for three different purposes : reading, writing and speaking.

Those who learn a foreign language may desire to learn it for all three purposes, or for one or two of them only. This work has been designed to enable the student to develop his powers as quickly and as easily as possible in all three. A language is a vast field, which can never be fully explored, and learning a language means hard work, careful thought and constant practice. If the student thinks he is going to speak or write or read German in a few months by means of a lesson or two done now and then, he had better give up the idea completely, for he is wasting his time. But this work, if followed conscientiously, will enable the average student not only to read German, but also to write and speak it in a fairly simple way.

The student without exceptional facilities must get into the habit of reading aloud, asking himself questions aloud and answering them himself—always, or as often as possible, aloud. The learning of words is important. To a large extent the vocabulary has been carefully kept up-to-date and thoroughly modern, with an eye to those who wish to read modern literature, to listen in to German broadcasts, or to travel on the Continent. These words should be mastered *somehow*, even if it means learning them off in lists. You must always have the subject in your mind. When you cast your eye on a thing, if you have known the German for it and forgotten, do not fail to look it up again at the *first* opportunity.

Conversational power is what you make it yourself. Not much has been given in actual conversations in this book, but all the exercises given are conversational in tone and subject matter. Make up your own conversations by rearranging the sentences given here.

A Key to the Exercises is given. This should be used sensibly. Do your exercise *before* consulting the Key, and then correct your own. Afterwards, do the exercises the other way round, testing your translation of the Key with the original exercises.

The student should revise constantly. In the scope of this little work it is impossible to give a thorough revision, but the student should, after every three lessons, go back and quickly refresh his mind on grammar and vocabulary.

As all the Exercises have their counterpart in the Key, no Vocabulary is given. But as many as possible of the words as they occur should be thoroughly committed to memory in order to render easier the task of translating subsequent exercises.

The section on Pronunciation is full and if the student follows it carefully he should have no difficulty in acquiring a fair pronunciation, if not a good one. If he can get native help so much the better.

One word of warning : we have kept all the exercises in this book within certain limits. We have attempted nothing very clever, nothing " high-falutin', " and you must also school yourselves to this. As soon as you start trying difficult constructions you will find yourselves in deep water. Keep your sentences fairly short and make sure of the matter given you here before attempting anything else.

If you would like to add a little reading of continuous German prose you could not do better than buy Guerber's *Märchen und Erzählungen*, Part I (Harrap), after the fourth or fifth lesson of this work. These Märchen, or tales, may strike you as childish, but if you can overcome this, you will find that the easy style and constant repetition will give you a confidence which is very important.

CONTENTS

CONTENTS

PART II

PART I

§ I. THE GERMAN ALPHABET

Some German books are still to be found with Gothic letters, although modern books and newspapers are printed in Roman type, and German typewriters are fitted with Roman letters. It would be useful, therefore, for the student to familiarize himself with the German alphabet (see pages 12 and 13) after he has worked through this book.

Note 1.—There are five vowels: a, e, i, o, u, and there are the further combinations ai (ai), au (au), ei (ai), eu (ɔi), ie (i).

Of the above, a, o, u and au may *modify*, *i.e.* change their sound. They are then written and pronounced: ä (ɛ), ö (ø or œ), ü (y), äu (ɔi). The two dots are referred to as the Umlaut, meaning a change of sound.

Note 2. There are several *digraphs* or *trigraphs*, *i.e.* groups of two or three consonants with a single sound:

ch	pronounced ç or x		ss	pronounced s	
ck	,,	k	sch	,,	ʃ
ph	,,	f	th	,,	t

N.B.—The following notes in this section refer to the Gothic letters only and should be left until the student has worked through this book. The student should now pass to page 15 and study the section on German pronunciation.

Note.—The small round s is used only at the end of a word, even if this word is the first part of a compound word:

> 𝔊las (glass), but 𝔊lafes (of a glass)
> bis (until) and bisher (until now)
> 𝔖taatsmann (statesman)

| English | German Characters | | Pronunciation[1] |
	Printed	Written	
A a (ä)	𝔄 a (ä)	𝒜 a	'ɑː ('ɛ)
B b	𝔅 b	ℒ b	beː
C c	ℭ c	ℒ c	tseː
D d	𝔇 d	𝒟 d	deː
E e	𝔈 e	ℰ e	'eː
F f	𝔉 f	ℱ f	'ɛf
G g	𝔊 g	𝒢 g	geː
H h	ℌ ħ	ℋ f	haː
I i	ℑ i	𝒥 i	'iː
J j	ℑ j	𝒥 j	jɔt
K k	𝔎 ɾ	𝒦 k	kɑː
L l	𝔏 l	ℒ l	'ɛl
M m	𝔐 m	ℳ m	'ɛm

[1] For the Pronunciation, see § 2, Preliminary Note.

| English | German Characters | | Pronunciation |
	Printed	Written	
N n	𝔑 n		'ɛn
O o (ö)	𝔒 o (ö)		'o: ('ø)
P p	𝔓 p		pe:
Q q	𝔔 q		ku:
R r	𝔑 r		'ɛr
S s	𝔖 ſ ß s		'ɛs
T t	𝔗 t		te:
U u (ü)	𝔘 u (ü)		'u: (y)
V v	𝔙 v		fau
W w	𝔚 w		ve:
X x	𝔛 x		'iks
Y y	𝔜 y		'ypsilɔn
Z z	𝖅 z		tsɛt

Note 4.—The double ſ is written ß (sz) at the end of a word or a syllable (when this syllable is not an integral part of the whole word but merely a prefix), and also after a long vowel and before a consonant :

muß, must   ißt, eats
eßbar, eatable, but eſſen, to eat
Fuß, foot   Kuß, kiss

Although the e in eßbar is short, the double ſ is written ß because at the end of a syllable, bar not being an integral part of the word, but an adjectival or adverbial suffix (-able).

In Fuß and Kuß, the u in the former is long and in the latter short, but both have ß because this is, as the above rule said, at the end of the word—*but* in the plural we have :

Füße (the double ſ not at the end but following a *long vowel*),
Küſſe (not ß because the vowel ü is short in this word, and the double ſ is not now at the end).

Observations.—In writing German with Roman characters the student may write Füße, or Füsse (as many Germans do), but if he keeps to the former, it will help to keep his pronunciation correct, *i.e.* to remember that the preceding vowel is long. There is no rule we can give for helping the student to know whether the vowel before a final ß in nouns is long or short. He must learn this by experience.

Note carefully these printed capital letters, which beginners are apt to confuse :

𝔅 (B) and 𝔙 (V)
ℭ (C), 𝔊 (G) and 𝔖 (S)
ℜ (R) and 𝔎 (K)
𝔒 (O) and 𝔔 (Q)

Also f (f) and ſ (s) (the f has the stroke right across, whereas the ſ has not).

Note carefully : b (b), d (d) and h (h).

Note also the difference in German written letters between :

ℳ (c) and ℐ (i, with dot)

ℳ (e, joining near top) and ℳ (n, joining at bottom)

ℳ (n) and ℳ (u, distinguished from n by stroke over it)

§ 2. GERMAN PRONUNCIATION

Preliminary Note

Before we go any further we must explain that the *symbols* we are using here to indicate the pronunciation are *symbols only and not ordinary German letters*. These symbols have been devised by the International Phonetic Association so that the pronunciation of all languages can be clearly explained by this International *Pronouncing* Alphabet. If you take the trouble to learn the sound-values of these symbols now you will be able to follow the phonetic transcription of any other language you undertake.

Practise your sounds aloud, clearly and continuously, and use a mirror to get your lip positions as indicated here.

A good pronunciation is well worth acquiring, and there is no reason why the average student who follows these notes conscientiously and continuously should not achieve this, although if he can obtain the help of a native or a good gramophone record on German pronunciation so much the better.

A Table of the Vowel-Sounds in German

Letter and Symbol	Nearest English Equivalent	Remarks
a { ɑ (long) [1] ɑ (short)	*a* as in *father* *a* as in *cast* said quickly : not as in *cat*	Almost like *u* in *must*.
e ɛ (long)	*ai* as in *fair*	There is no *er* sound at the end : it is one pure vowel-sound.
e ɛ (short)	*e* as in *bed*, *net*, *sent*	
e e (long)	*ee* as in *deep*	The teeth are not so close together as in the English *deep*. It is between the *ee* in *deep* and the *e* in *bed*.
e e (short)		As the preceding sound, but shorter.
i ɪ (always short)	*i* as in *bit*	
i i (long)	*ee* as in *deep*	The teeth are much closer together than in the English sound. The sound must almost be forced through.
o ɔ (always short)	*o* as in *not*	Morgen (mɔrgən)—*not* as in English Morgan.
o o (always long)	*aw* as in *lawn*	With lips *well rounded*. There is not the *o-oo* sound as in *bone*.
u { u (long) ʊ (short)	*oo* as in *ooze* *oo* as in *good*	Lips *well rounded* ! Lips *well rounded* !
ö œ (always short)	*ur* as in *fur* (*r* not being pronounced).	Lips *must be well rounded*, as for ɔ.
ö ø (always long)	No equivalent in English. It is the same as the French *eu* in *feu*	Pronounce the preceding sound, closing the mouth somewhat and keeping the lips rounded as for ɔ.

[1] A long vowel is indicated in the pronunciation by a colon (:).

Table of the Vowel-Sounds in German—*continued*

Letter and Symbol	Nearest English Equivalent	Remarks
ü y (long)	No equivalent in English. Almost like the French *u* as in *sur*	Put your lips as for whistling (position as for u) and try to say *ee*. The German grün (gryn) is like the English *green* with the lips kept as for whistling.
ü ʏ (short)	No English equivalent.	As the preceding sound, but *short*. The German Müller is like the English *miller* with the lips as for whistling.
e ə	*a* as in *ago*, *er* as in *further*.	A short sound, that of unaccented e.

Table of the Consonant-Sounds in German

Where no note is given the reader is to assume that the German consonant has the same sound as in English.

Letter and Symbol	Nearest English Equivalent	Remarks
b b	*b* as in *bed*	
b p	*p* as in *put*	Only when *b* stands at end of word or syllable.
c ts		ts pronounced as one sound : practise the " English " *that's 'im !* This is the sound of c before e, i, ö or ä. Has largely given way to z.
c k		The sound of c otherwise, although has largely given way to k.
ch k		In words from the Greek (Charakter).

Table of Consonant-Sounds in German—*continued*

Letter and Symbol	Nearest English Equivalent	Remarks
ch ç	*h* in *huge*	Exaggerate the *h* in *huge*. Force the tongue against roof of mouth.
ch x	Scots *loch*	Whereas ç is pronounced at front of mouth, x is pronounced in the throat. Say *lock* forcing the air through on the *k*. This is the pronunciation of ch only after a, o or u.
d d	*d* as in *dead*	
d t	*t* as in *tomb*	This is the pronunciation of d at end of word or syllable.
g g	*g* as in *go*	Always, except as under.
g ʒ	*s* as in *casual*	Only in a few French words (Courage, kurɑ:ʒə).
g k		At end of word or syllable except when preceded by n : Tag (tɑk).
g ç		In -ig, except when followed by -lich : Sonnig (zɔnɪç), but : Königlich (kønɪglɪç).
h h	*h* as in *hand*	*Always* pronounced before a vowel.
j j	*y* as in *yes*	
l l	*l* as in *lump*	Put tip of tongue between top teeth and gum.
ng ŋ	*ng* as in *sing*	Always : never pronounce *g* as in *finger*.
ph f		In words from Greek. Mostly replaced now by f.
qu kv		Quelle (kvɛlə).
r r		Is trilled more than in English, although scarcely heard in ending -er.
s s	*s* as in *soap*	At end of word or syllable only : Glas (glɑ:s).
s z	*z* as in *zeal*	Only at beginning of word or syllable : Seife (zɑifə), Rose (ro:zə).

Table of Consonant-Sounds in German—*continued*

Letter and Symbol	Nearest English Equivalent	Remarks
S s ʃ	*sh* as in *sharp*	Before p or t only : Speise (ʃpaizə), Stern (ʃtɛrn), sparen (ʃpɑːrən).
ss s	*s* as in *soap*	
sch ʃ	*sh* as in *sharp*	
v f	*f* as in *far*	Except in a few French words (Vase, vɑːzə).
w v	*v* as in *vat*	
y j	*y* as in *yes*	Only when a consonant : Yukka (jʊkkɑ).
y { y (short) / y (long) / i		Does not often occur as a vowel.
z ts		See c above; z is always so pronounced.

Observations.—There are no silent letters as in English. Thus, although we say *knave*, the Germans say Knabe (knɑːbə), both the k and the e being pronounced.

h is not pronounced between two vowels unless the h is part of the following syllable : sehen (zeən), but : Hoheit (hohait).

chs when part of the word itself (the s not being added for some grammatical reason) is pronounced ks : sechs (zɛks), Ochs (ɔks), wachsen (vɑksən), etc.

The Glottal Stop is what the phoneticians mean by the forced stop between one word or syllable and a following one beginning with an accented or stressed vowel. Let us consider the English expression *fresh eggs*. We carry the *sh* sound straight on : fresheggs. But the equivalent German expression is not so pronounced. There is a pause after frische, the vocal organs contract, and the following word begins after a complete break between the two with an almost explosive force : frische Eier.

This is not entirely unknown in English. A Cockney will sometimes say, for instance, *Git aht o' 'ere*, the expression not being smoothly carried on, but rather awkwardly broken up.

The Glottal Stop is written phonetically?

The Stress in German

The German spoken language is strongly stressed. You have only to listen in to a German broadcast to realize that. The following rules will be more helpful later on, but in the meantime the stress will be indicated by a mark ' after the stressed syllable.

1. The stress is laid on the *stem* of the word :

geh'-en, ge-fähr'-lich, Mäd'-chen

(The principal parts in these words being geh, fähr, Mäd).

2. In compound words the stress is usually on the first part :

Turm'-uhr, eis'-kalt, Va'ter-land

But not with the adverbial particles: hin-ein', da-mit', etc.

3. Separable prefixes take the main stress :

aus'-gehen, hin-auf'-klettern, her-un'ter-kommen

4. The negative prefix un- is always stressed :

un'-artig, Un'-sinn, un'-erwartet

A Simple Exercise in Reading

The following passage is given first in Roman type, next in German Fraktur type, thirdly in phonetic script, fourthly in German handwriting, and finally English.

Practise the pronunciation carefully, referring constantly to the foregoing notes.

Roman Type

Der Winter ist kalt. Es regnet oft und es schneit manchmal. Dann sind die Dächer der Häuser mit Schnee bedeckt. Der Schnee ist weiss und schön. Die Jungen und Mädchen spielen gern mit dem Schnee. Manchmal sind die Flüsse und Teiche zugefroren. Dann nehmen die jungen Leute ihre Schlittschuhe und sie gehen auf das Eis. Dort haben sie viel Spass. Wenn aber das Tauwetter eintritt, ist es gefährlich, auf das Eis zu gehen.

German Fraktur

Der Winter ist kalt. Es regnet oft und es schneit manchmal. Dann sind die Dächer der Häuser mit Schnee bedeckt. Der Schnee ist weiß und schön. Die Jungen und Mädchen spielen gern mit dem Schnee. Manchmal sind die Flüsse und Teiche zugefroren. Dann nehmen die jungen Leute ihre Schlittschuhe und sie gehen auf das Eis. Dort haben sie viel Spaß. Wenn aber das Tauwetter eintritt, ist es gefährlich, auf das Eis zu gehen.

Phonetic Version

der vin'tər ʔist kalt. ɛs reg'nət ɔft ʔunt ʔes ʃnait manç'maːl. dan zint di dɛ'çər der hɔi'zər mit ʃneː bədɛkt'. der ʃneː': ʔist vais unt ʃøːn. di juˈŋən ʔunt mɛt'çən ʃpiː'lən gɛrn mit dɛm ʃneː manç'maːl zint di flyˈsə ʔunt tai'çə tsu'gəfroˈrən. dan ne'ːmən di juˈŋən lɔi'tə iːrə ʃlit'ʃuːə ʔunt zi ge'ːən auf das ʔais. dɔrt ha'ːbən zi fiːl ʃpaːs. vɛn ʔaːbər das tau'wɛtər ʔaintrit, ʔist ʔes gəfɛːr'liç, auf das ʔais tsu ge'ːən.

The following is given as a rough guide, although the student, if he seriously wishes to acquire a good pronunciation, must read and re-read the foregoing rules, and practise continually the previous phonetic version :

dair vinter ist kahlt. es reegnert (ert *very short !*) oft unt (u *as oo in book, not as u in but*) es shnite (*to rhyme with kite*) manchmahl. dahnn zint dee decher (deHer, H *as in huge*) dair hoyzer mit schnee berdeckt (ber *very short !*). dair shnee ist vice unt shern (*lips rounded !*). dee yungen unt met-Hern (ern *very short !*) shpeelern (ern *very short !*) gairn mit dem shnee. manH-mahl zint die flisser (i *pronounced with rounded lips !*) unt tie-Her tsoogefroren (*stress on* tsoo *and* fror). Etc.

German Handwriting

English Version

The winter is cold. It rains often and snows some-times. Then are the roofs of-the houses with snow covered. The snow is white and beautiful. The boys and girls play gladly with the snow. Sometimes are the rivers and ponds over-frozen. Then take the young people their skates and go on-to the ice. There have they much fun. When the thaw-weather in-steps (sets in), is it dangerous on the ice to go.

LESSON I

THE SIMPLE SENTENCE

1. The Masculine Nouns

We now come to the study of the language itself. The name of any person or thing is called a noun. Thus *apple* and *tailor* are nouns.

Apple is singular, *apples* is plural.

The plural of nouns in German is formed in different ways. After all, we have, in addition to *apple, apples*, such plurals as *ox, oxen, man, men, woman, women, sheep, sheep, child, children*. We see in some of these plurals a change of vowel sound: *man, men; woman* (wʊmən), *women* (wɪmɪn), etc. This change of vowel sound, or Umlaut, as the Germans call it, occurs in the plural of many German nouns, but not all.

All German nouns, whether representing persons or things, are *masculine, feminine* or *neuter*, whereas in English things are usually neuter, although we often say *she* of a ship and other things. The *gender*, or sex, as it were, of a noun is very important, as the word for *the* (which is always the same in English) changes according to the gender. The student must therefore learn every noun with the article (*the*) before it. Thus it is not only necessary to know that *apple* is Apfel in German: he must know it is der Apfel.

In this first section we are going to deal only with masculine nouns ending in -el, -en or -er.

In the following list notice which nouns have the Umlaut in the plural and which have not. Notice also that the plural form of der (*the*) is die (the).

Notice further that *all nouns* are written with a capital letter in German.

Singular	Plural
der Garten, garden	die Gärten
der Apfel, apple	die Äpfel
der Schneider, tailor	die Schneider
der Bruder, brother	die Brüder
der Vater, father	die Väter
der Lehrer, teacher	die Lehrer
der Schüler, schoolboy	die Schüler
der Onkel, uncle	die Onkel
der Bäcker, baker	die Bäcker
der Laden, shop	die Läden
der Wagen, cart, carriage, motor-car	die Wagen

Notice that Schneider, Lehrer have no Umlaut in the plural because e's and i's cannot take one. Of the others only Onkel and Wagen have no Umlaut in the plural, and Schüler and Bäcker have the Umlaut already in the singular.

Vocabulary

er, he	schön, beautiful
sie, they	ehrlich, honest
ist, is	unehrlich, dishonest
sind, are	ja, yes
nicht, not	nein, no
dort, there	manchmal, sometimes
hier, here	immer, always
gut, good	oft, often
schlecht, bad	freundlich, friendly
arm, poor	böse, angry, wicked
reich, rich	ganz, quite

Exercise 1

Read and then turn into English:

Der Bruder ist arm. Der Vater ist nicht schlecht. Ist der Onkel hier? Nein, er ist dort. Ist der Laden nicht hier? Ja, er[1] ist hier. Der Bäcker ist oft ganz unehrlich. Der Schüler ist manchmal böse. Ist der Apfel nicht gut? Nein, er ist schlecht. Ist der Garten

[1] Note that, as these words are masculine, even though some of them refer to things the English *it* must in all these cases become er (*he*) in German.

schön? Ja, er ist schön. Ist der Lehrer immer freundlich? Nein, er ist manchmal böse. Ist der Onkel arm?
Nein, er ist ganz reich.

Exercise 2

Turn the above sentences into the plural. Remember
that the adjective after the verb *is* or *are* does not change.
We will show you by doing the first one: Die Brüder sind
arm. When you have completed the exercise (but not
before) turn to the Key beginning page 151 and see
whether you have made any mistakes.

2. The Feminine Nouns [Monosyllables]

We are now going to deal with a number of feminine
monosyllables (words of one syllable). Notice that the
word for *the* is die in both the singular and the plural.
All these words have the Umlaut in the plural (except
where the vowel is e or i) and take -e as their plural
ending:

Singular	Plural
die Stadt, city, town	die Städte
die Nacht, night	die Nächte
die Hand, hand	die Hände
die Kuh, cow	die Kühe
die Magd, maid	die Mägde
die Maus, mouse	die Mäuse
die Nuss, nut	die Nüsse
die Wand, wall	die Wände
die Wurst, sausage	die Würste

Vocabulary

dunkel, dark	klein, little, short
schwarz, black	dick, fat, thick
braun, brown	sehr, very
weiss, white	dünn, thin
fertig, ready	hungrig, hungry
sie, she, they	durstig, thirsty
reif, ripe	alt, old
sauer, sour	neu, new
gross, big, tall	und, and

Exercise 3

Read and then turn into English:

Die Stadt ist sehr alt. Ist die Nuss reif? Die Kuh ist nicht braun. Die Magd ist nicht sehr gross. Ist die Nacht nicht dunkel? Ist die Wurst fertig? Die Wand ist sehr schön. Ist die Hand braun? Nein, sie ist weiss. Ist die Kuh durstig? Nein, sie ist hungrig. Die Stadt ist nicht alt, sie ist neu. Ist die Maus immer klein? Die Magd ist manchmal sehr freundlich. Die Nuss ist alt und sauer. Die Nacht ist ganz schwarz. Die Magd ist gross und dünn.

Exercise 4

Turn the above exercise into the plural, afterwards comparing it with the answers in the Key (see page 152).

3. The Neuter Nouns

Now we come to the third and last gender. *Neuter* is a Latin word meaning *neither, i.e.* neither masculine nor feminine. Notice that in this case the singular definite article is das (*the*), while the plural is, as for the masculine and feminine, again die. These neuter nouns we give here all take the Umlaut in the plural (except where the vowel is e or i) and the plural ending is -er.

Singular	Plural
das Blatt, leaf	die Blätter
das Buch, book	die Bücher
das Dach, roof	die Dächer
das Dorf, village	die Dörfer
das Ei, egg	die Eier
das Feld, field	die Felder
das Glas, glass	die Gläser
das Haus, house	die Häuser
das Horn, horn	die Hörner
das Kind, child	die Kinder
das Kleid, dress	die Kleider
das Lied, song	die Lieder
das Rad, wheel	die Räder
das Wort, word	die Wörter

Vocabulary

lang, long	viereckig, square
kurz, short	hoch, high
voll, full	niedrig, low
leer, empty	sie, they
grün, green	aber, but
rot, red	oder, or
es, it	ziemlich, fairly
schwer, difficult *Heavy.*	fast, almost, nearly
leicht, easy	zu, too
rund, round	selten, seldom

Exercise 5

Read and then translate into English:

Das Lied ist nicht sehr schön. Das Rad ist rund. Ist das Dorf nicht klein und sehr alt? Das Ei ist nicht rund. Das Dach ist rot. Das Buch ist nicht zu schwer. Ist das Glas nicht leer? Nein, es ist fast zu voll. Ist das Wort leicht? Nein, es ist sehr lang und schwer. Ist das Kind gross? Nein, es ist sehr klein. Das Haus ist ziemlich hoch. Ist das Feld rund oder viereckig? Es ist viereckig. Das Kleid ist ganz neu, aber es ist nicht sehr schön. Das Blatt ist lang und grün. Ist das Haus nicht zu niedrig?

Exercise 6

Turn the above exercise into the plural, and then compare your answers with the Key.

Revision Exercise

Translate into German:

Are the gardens long and beautiful? They are beautiful, but they are not very long. Is the tailor always honest? Yes, he is always honest. Is the glass always full? No, it is often empty. Are the cities old or new? They are old. The fields are nearly always green. Are

the nuts not ripe? The apples are too green and sour.
Is the house big or small? It is very big. Are the shops
always empty? No, they are seldom empty. Are the
maids tall and thin? No, they are short and fat. Are
the children always good? No, they are sometimes
very wicked. The night is long and very dark. The
brother is poor but quite honest, and the father is rich but
quite dishonest. The songs are too long and too difficult.
Here is the village, and there is the house. The child is
nearly always hungry.

LESSON II

THE WEAK VERB

Pronouns are little words which are used to avoid the
repetition of nouns, and a few English pronouns are:
I, you, we, us, them, it.

Pronouns are divided into persons and numbers.
There are three persons:

First person: the person speaking (*I, we, me, us*).
Second person: the person addressed (*you*).
Third person: the person spoken about (*he, she, it,
they, him, her, them*).

The numbers are singular (one person, as *I, you, he,
she, it*) and plural (as *we, you, they*).

As in English we must say *I am, he is, we are*, and it is
wrong to say *we is, he am, they loves*, etc., so in German
there are certain endings to the verb (the word which
expresses a *state* or an *action*, as *am, do, love, hate*, etc.)
and these endings must be learnt carefully by heart,
and must never be confused.

Let us look at the following conjugation, or arrange-
ment of the verb:

lieben, *to love*

Singular		Plural	
ich liebe	I love	wir lieben	we love
du liebst	you love	ihr liebt	you love
er ⎫	he ⎫		
sie ⎬liebt	she ⎬loves	⎰ sie lieben	they love
es ⎭	it ⎭		
Sie lieben	you love	Sie lieben	you love

First of all, let us explain the various forms meaning *you love*.

Du is used to one person with whom one is very friendly and intimate. It is also used by grown-ups to a young child, and it is used always to address an animal. It may also be used to express contempt. Du is only written with a capital letter in correspondence.

Ihr is the form used in the above circumstances when more than one person, child or animal is being addressed.

Sie (always written with a capital) is used in all other cases. It is the ordinary form of address, and the only one likely to be used by the average English person just staying in Germany for a short time. He might risk du on a small child or a dog, but let him beware of using du to anybody else! Sie means *you* whether one person only is addressed or several, and the verb ending (-en) is the same in both cases.

The one who is something or does something is called the *subject*. When the subject is a noun the verb has the same ending as the pronouns *he* or *they*:

Der Bruder ⎫	⎫	The brother ⎫	⎫
Er ⎬liebt	⎬	He ⎬loves	⎬
Die Brüder ⎫	⎫	The brothers ⎫	⎫
Sie ⎬lieben	⎬	They ⎬love	⎬

The student must therefore see that his verb ending is the correct one for the subject: thus in the verb lieben, to love, to the stem lieb- are added endings as follows:

```
ich has the verb ending in -e      —    ich liebe
du    ,,     ,,             ,,  -st (-est) *du liebst
```

er ⎫		er liebt
sie ⎬ have the verb ending in -t (-et) * ⎨		sie liebt
es ⎪		es liebt
ihr ⎭		ihr liebt
wir ⎫		wir lieben
sie ⎬ ,, ,, ,, -en ⎨		sie lieben
Sie ⎭		Sie lieben

Note.—With the -st (-est) and -t (-et) endings the extra e is put in when the *stem* of the verb (*i.e.* that part left when the endings are taken away) ends in a consonant followed by d, t, m or n, in the du, er and ihr forms; and when the stem ends in a hissing consonant (s, z, ss) the extra e is kept in the du form only.

Examples (using the verbs öffnen, landen, atmen, zeichnen, reisen, tanzen):

du öffnest (you open), er landet (he lands), du atmest (you breathe), er zeichnet (he draws);

du reisest (you travel), but: er reist (he travels);

du tanzest (you dance), but: ihr tanzt (you dance)

Notice further that verbs whose infinitive (or simplest) form ends in -ern or -eln have -ere and -le after ich, and -ert and -elt after er or ihr:

ändern, to change:

ich ändere,	I change
du änderst,	you change
er ändert,	he changes

lächeln, to smile:

ich lächle,	I smile
du lächelst,	you smile
er lächelt,	he smiles

Asking a Question

The interrogative form is quite simple. The English *do* or *does* in such forms as *Do I smoke? Does she dance? Do you telephone? Does the man travel?* do not exist in German. The German question form is always *Smoke I? Dances she? Telephone you? Travels the man?* etc. Thus:

Do I smoke?	Rauche ich?
Does she dance?	Tanzt sie?
Do you telephone?	Telefonieren Sie?
Does the man travel?	Reist der Mann?

The Negative Form

We also use *do* and *does* in making a negative statement. The Germans never do this, but say quite simply *I smoke not, she dances not*, etc.

I do not smoke	Ich rauche nicht.
She does not dance.	Sie tanzt nicht.
You do not telephone.	Sie telefonieren nicht.
The man does not travel.	Der Mann reist nicht.

Vocabulary

träumen, to dream	machen, to make
atmen, to breathe	kochen, to boil
reisen, to travel	spielen, to play
zeichnen, to draw	sagen, to say
lieben, to love	antworten, to answer
hassen, to hate	lachen, to laugh
schicken, to send	lächeln, to smile
telefonieren, to telephone	suchen, to seek, look for
rauchen, to smoke	hören, to hear
arbeiten, to work	weinen, to weep
reichen, to hand, pass	besuchen, to visit
öffnen, to open	

Exercise 7

Put the following into the plural, thus:

Ich träume	wir träumen
Du tanzest	ihr tanzt
Er raucht	sie rauchen
Der Schneider arbeitet	die Schneider arbeiten

Ich besuche. Du suchst. Er sagt. Telefoniert sie? Der Bruder lacht. Die Magd kocht. Spielt der Schüler? Du sagst. Ich höre. Sie hasst. Sie (you) suchen.

Exercise 8

Put the following into the singular:

Träumen wir? Ihr antwortet. Sie (they, masc.) zeichnen. Die Onkel reisen. Die Kinder atmen. Hören Sie (you)? Sie (they, fem.) arbeiten. Die Brüder hassen. Wir lächeln. Antworten die Lehrer?

Exercise 9

Translate into German:

(*a*) I hear the cow. The uncle hates the maid. The maids boil the sausages. We love the maid. You (du, *or 2nd sing.*) look for the nuts. The tailors make the dresses. The brother visits the village. I pass the glasses. The children hate the song. She draws the house. I smile, but she weeps. /

(*b*) We look for the cows. I hear the mice. Do you (Sie) send the books? Does she smoke? Do you (Sie) not dance? Does the father work? Do the children play? Is the maid boiling [1] the leaves? Am I dreaming? Are you (*2nd sing.*) weeping? Is the child breathing?

LESSON III

THE CASES

We said before that the person or thing which is or does something is the *Subject*. The *Subject* is always in what is called the *Nominative Case*. This is so in English, but it does not matter much to us, as our words do not change much, but it is important in German.

When the action of the verb passes directly on to somebody or something else, that somebody or something is the *Direct Object*, and is in the *Accusative Case*.

If we take the sentence *The tailor makes the dress*, and ask: *Who makes the dress?* we get the answer *The tailor*. The tailor is there the Subject and in the Nominative Case. If we ask: *What does he make?* we get the answer *The dress*. The dress is therefore the Direct Object, in the Accusative Case.

In Exercise 9 we successfully did a number of sentences

---

[1] I am working = I work.
Am I working ? = work I ?

M.   F.   N.   Pl.
m *der die das*   *die*
den die das   *die*
des der des THE CASES   **33**
dem der dem   *der*
                                   den

like this without needing to know anything about cases. But that was because the sentences were carefully chosen to avoid difficulties. If you go back to that exercise you will find that no masculine singular nouns occurred in the Direct Object or Accusative Case, because der (Nominative singular) becomes den (Accusative singular), although the feminine singular, neuter singular and the plural forms (die, das and die) remain the same.

We will now do an exercise including some masculine singular nouns in the Accusative Case. Compare the following:

> Der Bruder arbeitet
> Ich besuche den Bruder.

In the first sentence, who works? The brother— therefore the Nominative Case.

In the second sentence, whom do I visit? The brother —therefore in the Accusative.

Exercise 10

Besuchst du den Onkel? Ich suche die Eier. Der Bruder besucht den Laden. Der Schneider reicht das Kleid. Der Lehrer sucht den Schüler. Wir hören die Schüler. Der Bäcker schickt die Würste. Die Magd kocht den Apfel. Sie kocht Äpfel.

Exercise 11

Do you [1] hear the song? I visit the brother. We look for the teacher. The schoolboy looks for eggs. I draw the house. The teacher says the word. The father visits the uncle. She does not answer. Does the uncle visit the town? You (du) visit the baker.

There is another kind of object, the *Indirect Object*. This might be said to answer the question *To whom?*

[1] Use Sie unless told differently.

B

suchen = to look for
besuchen = to visit

Consider the sentence:

The tailor sends the baker the apples.

Who sends?	The tailor.	(Nominative Case.)
What does he send?	The apples.	(Accusative Case.)
To whom does he send?	To the baker.	(Dative Case.)

Very often the Dative Case is expressed in English by *to*: The tailor sends the apples to the baker. But as this *to* does not imply physical motion towards, but a receiving of something, the *to* is not expressed in German, the Dative Case of the article and the noun being sufficient.

The Dative Case of the Article is as follows:

Singular			Plural
Masc.	Fem.	Neut.	M., F. and N.
dem	der	dem	den *(dane)*

N.B. In the case of two nouns, the Dative precedes the Accusative, no matter what the English order may be.

Exercise 12

Der Onkel reicht dem Vater die Nüsse. Die Magd schickt dem Bruder die Äpfel. Der Vater antwortet [1] dem Schneider. Der Bäcker schickt dem Lehrer Nüsse und Äpfel. Du reichst dem Vater den Apfel. Wir schicken der Magd Bücher und Kleider. Ich reiche dem Kind das Ei.

Exercise 13

The teacher sends the father the book. The maid passes the nuts to the uncle. The schoolboys hand the books to the teacher. We send eggs and apples to the maid. The schoolboy answers the father. The maid hands the dress to the tailor. I pass the glass to the baker. You answer the teacher.

Sometimes a noun is put next to another noun in a descriptive sense, to express ownership. Thus we said

---

[1] The meaning is: *replies to.*

in English *the uncle's book* or *the book of the uncle*. The thing we are really talking about is the book, and we add *uncle's* or *of the uncle* to describe which book. The case of this expression *uncle's* or *of the uncle* is called Possessive in English, and in German it is referred to as the Genitive Case. The noun in the Genitive Case usually (but not always) follows the noun on which it depends, and the Definite Article is also put into the Genitive Case.

The Genitive Case of the Definite Article is as follows:

Singular			Plural
Masc.	Fem.	Neut.	M., F. and N.
des	der	des	der

Of the nouns that we have used up till now the *feminines take no ending* in the Genitive singular, the masculines in -el, -en, -er take s and the neuters take -es. In the plural they all have the same endings as for the Nominative plural.

Masc. des Lehrers, of the teacher   der Lehrer, of the teachers
Fem. der Magd, of the maid   der Mägde, of the maids
Neut. des Blattes, of the leaf   der Blätter, of the leaves

Position of nicht in the sentence

Nicht (Not) is usually placed after the direct object, although in a question it often comes after the verb:

Er schickt die Äpfel nicht.   He does not send the apples.
Schickt er nicht dem Bäcker die Äpfel?   Does he not send the apples to the baker?

Exercise 14

Der Laden des Bäckers ist schön und neu. Die Kühe des Onkels sind gross und braun. Die Räder des Wagens sind rund. Das Kleid der Magd ist rot. Die Wände des Hauses sind weiss. Die Häuser der Dörfer sind klein. Das Glas des Kindes ist leer. Der Lehrer öffnet die Bücher der Schüler. Der Bruder des Schneiders schickt der Magd des Vaters das Kleid. Hörst du nicht die Lieder der Kinder? Ich telefoniere dem Vater des Bäckers. Die Magd des Schneiders schickt dem Bruder des Bäckers Äpfel und Nüsse. Die Hörner der Kuh sind nicht sehr lang. Die Hände der Magd sind klein und weiss, aber die Hände der Brüder sind ganz gross und rot.

Exercise 15

Remember that of two noun objects, the Indirect (Dative) usually precedes the Direct (Accusative).

The horns of the cows are not too long. I telephone to the brother of the maid. The roof of the house is square and red. The schoolboy's father answers the teacher. The uncle's maid sends eggs and apples to the tailor's brother. Does he not visit the tailor of the village? Do you not hear the maid's song? The bakers' shops are quite full. The baker's brother hears the songs of the children. I do not send the maid's dress to the tailor.

LESSON IV

HABEN, SEIN AND THE IMPERFECT

Nearly all masculine nouns ending in e form all their cases except the Nominative sing. by simply adding n. Thus Knabe, a boy:

	Singular	Plural
Nom.	der Knabe	die Knaben
Acc.	den Knaben	die Knaben
Gen.	des Knaben	der Knaben
Dat.	dem Knaben	den Knaben

Note that there is no Umlaut.

There are two verbs that you cannot learn too soon or too well. Here they are: haben, to have, and sein, to be.

Present of haben

Singular		Plural	
1. ich habe	I have	wir haben	we have
2. du hast	thou hast	{Sie haben / ihr habt }	you have
3. er hat	he has	sie haben	they have

Observe that haben is a little irregular so far as we know it yet. Sein is quite irregular.

Present of sein

Singular		Plural	
1. ich bin	I am	wir sind	we are
2. du bist	thou art	{Sie sind / ihr seid }	you are
3. er ist	he is	sie sind	they are

So far we have been dealing with the *Present tense*, that is, our verbs have dealt only with things now going on. In dealing with things that were done in the past we use a form of verb called the *Imperfect tense*. It is easily learned, and differs from the Present in having a t all through, and in having a final e in the third person singular. Compare the following with the Present of lieben as given on page 29:

Imperfect Indicative of lieben

Singular		Plural	
1. ich liebte	I loved	wir liebten	we loved *lieben*
2. du liebtest	thou lovedst	{Sie liebten / ihr liebtet }	you loved *liebt*
3. er liebte	he loved	sie liebten	they loved *lieben*

(margin notes: ebe, bst, bt.)

The Imperfect may be put into English in two ways: (1) *I loved*, (2) *I was loving*. Ich liebte does duty for both forms. In English we often use *do* and *is*, and *was* and *did* along with verbs. *I am loving, you were loving*, etc., are called the *progressive* form, because they show

that the loving is or was going on continuously: *I do love,
she did love*, etc., are called the emphatic form. But
German does not allow this use of *am, was, do, did*;
these little words are NEVER put into German along with
verbs. I do love is just ich liebe. I am loving is just
the same, ich liebe. Do I love? = liebe ich? Am I
loving? is the same, liebe ich? I was loving = ich
liebte. I did love = ich liebte. Did I love = liebte
ich? She is loving = sie liebt. Does she love? = liebt
sie?

Vocabulary *zeichnen – to chan*

der Neffe, nephew	leben, to live, be alive
der Löwe, lion	lernen, to learn
der Franzose, Frenchman	erzählen, to tell, relate
der Hase, hare	wohnen, to dwell, live
der Ochse, ox	wo? where?
der Matrose, sailor	oben, upstairs
der Junge, boy	unten, downstairs
tot, dead	noch, still

Exercise 16

Wir sind Franzosen. Wo wohnen die Brüder des
Matrosen? Sie wohnen nicht hier. Erzähltest du dem
Jungen das Lied der Matrosen? Sind die Neffen des
Franzosen oben? Nein, sie sind unten. Leben die
Hasen des Knaben? Nein, sie sind tot. Die Jungen
zeichneten die Löwen. Lernten Sie nicht das Lied des
Matrosen? Wir besuchten nicht oft den Neffen des
Franzosen. Die Hörner des Ochsen sind sehr lang. Sie
schickten den Matrosen Äpfel, Nüsse und Eier.

Exercise 17

Where do you live? Does the hare still live (= live
still)? No, it is dead. Did you send the boy's book
to the baker's nephew? Where is the sailor's house?
It is there. Where are the Frenchman's oxen? They
are not here. Is not the Frenchmen's house white? No,

it is red; there is the roof of the house. Is the sailor's
nephew not learning the song? Was the Frenchman's
nephew smoking? No, he was not smoking, he was
working. Are the sailor's children playing? I was
laughing, but she was weeping. Did you live upstairs
or downstairs?

Exercise 18

We are poor, but you are rich. Marie is upstairs and
Peter is playing downstairs. Gretchen and Paula have
the hare. It is big and brown. Has the sailor the ox?
Are you (du) still there? Yes, I am here. Have the
sailors glasses? Yes, they have glasses, but they are
empty. Where are we? We are upstairs. Where are
the sailor's nephews playing? They are there. Have
you (du) cows and oxen? No, but I have the hare.

Conversational Expressions

Guten Morgen !	Good morning !
Guten Abend !	Good evening !
Guten Tag !	Good day !
Gute Nacht !	Good night !
Wie geht es Ihnen ?	How are you ?
Sehr gut, danke, und Ihnen ?	Very well, thank you, and you ?

LESSON V

THE DEMONSTRATIVE ADJECTIVES—SOME PREPOSITIONS

Imperfect of sein

Singular		Plural	
1. ich war	I was	wir waren	we were
2. du warst	thou wast	{ Sie waren / ihr wart }	you were
3. er war	he was	sie waren	they were

Imperfect of haben

	Singular		Plural	
1.	ich hatte	I had	wir hatten	we had
2.	du hattest	thou hadst	{ Sie hatten / ihr hattet }	you had
3.	er hatte	he had	sie hatten	they had

Exercise 19

Die Nüsse und Äpfel waren nicht reif. Der Neffe des Lehrers war oben. Die Brüder der Magd waren tot. Die Kühe des Onkels waren gross und braun. Ich hatte den Hasen, aber er ist tot. War der Vater des Schülers sehr böse? Nein, er war ziemlich freundlich. War das Glas des Matrosen leer? Nein, es war ganz voll. Hattest du den Garten? Ja, er war sehr schön. Wo warst du? Ich war oben.

Exercise 20

Where was the sailor? He was not here. Were the teachers there? Yes, and the scholars. Was the teacher always friendly? No, he was often very angry. Did you have the house there? Yes, we had the house and the garden. Were the sausages ready? No, but we had apples and nuts. I was very thirsty and the glass was quite empty.

The Definite Article and the Demonstratives

It is better to learn the article, as you have been doing, by using it. But since we have now seen it in all its forms, it may be well to gather it up into one table for reference.

	Singular			Plural
	Masc.	Fem.	Neut.	M., F. and N.
Nom.	der	die	das	die
Acc.	den	die	das	die
Gen.	des	der	des	der
Dat.	dem	der	dem	den

There is another reason for giving the article in full here. There are certain little words called *demonstratives* that are used to point out nouns in German, and these are declined exactly like der, die, das. These words are dieser = this; jener = that; jeder = every. With the three genders they appear:

Singular			Plural
Masc.	Fem.	Neut.	M., F. and N.
dieser	diese	dieses	diese
jener	jene	jenes	jene
jeder	jede	jedes	alle

[handwritten margin notes: his, hat, very]

The very meaning of the word shows us that we cannot have a plural of jeder; we use alle instead. We cannot say *every houses*, but we can say *all houses*: alle Häuser.

Another word, which does not point out but asks a question, is declined in the same way. It is welcher, welche, welches (sing.), welche (plural). It means *which ?*

Thus: dieser Ochse = this ox; jene Kuh = that cow; jedes Buch = every book; welches Buch? = which book?

Some Prepositions

Prepositions are little words like *to*, *with* or *in*, which show the relation between certain words in sentences. In English prepositions are said to govern the Accusative Case, but in German they may govern the Accusative, the Dative or the Genitive Case. We shall begin with six which govern the *Dative*.

[handwritten note: GOVERN DATIVE]

aus, out	in,[1] in
mit, with	von, of or from
nach, after or to	zu, to or at

Thus we write: aus dem Hause = out of the house, in der Stadt = in the town, nach dem Lehrer = after the teacher, zu Hause = at the house or at home.

[1] *In* can *also* govern the Accusative : but in the meantime we shall use it only with the Dative.

Vocabulary

eins, one	elf, eleven	der Krieg, war
zwei, two	zwölf, twelve	das Zimmer, room
drei, three	dreizehn, thirteen	die Kirche, church
vier, four	vierzehn, fourteen	das Geschäft, business
fünf, five	fünfzehn, fifteen	die Schule, school
sechs, six	sechzehn, sixteen	die Klasse, class
sieben, seven	siebzehn, seventeen	es war, there (-it) was
acht, eight	achtzehn, eighteen	es waren, there (-it) were
neun, nine	neunzehn, nineteen	
zehn, ten	zwanzig, twenty	

Exercise 21

Welches Kind spielt in dem Garten? Dieses Kind spielt in dem Garten mit dem Neffen des Schneiders. Waren [1] zehn Kühe in jenem Feld? Nein, es waren acht Ochsen dort. Jeder Schüler hatte vier Bücher. In welcher Klasse bist du? Ich bin in dieser Klasse. Waren Sie sehr arm nach dem Krieg? Der Bäcker schickte den Neffen aus dem Zimmer. In welchem Dorf wohnten Sie? Wir wohnten in diesem Dorf, in jenem Haus dort.

Exercise 22

Had every child five or six apples? Which teacher sent the father this book? The three children were in the church. I sent the children to (the) school. Were there eight or nine houses in that village? There were seven. There are (es sind) five teachers in this school, and there are ten children in each class. In which house do you live? Which song did you learn? Which boy did you send out of the class? Which cow did you hear? He sent nine eggs with the dress. Every child in that village has three or four books. In which room is the sailor's nephew? He is upstairs in the uncle's room.

[1] Notice that when war or waren comes first, the es is omitted.

Conversation

Bitte, reichen Sie mir jenen Hut !	Please pass me that hat.
Hier ist er.	Here it is.
Danke vielmals !	Many thanks.
Bitte schön.	Not at all.
Bitte, wo ist die Post ?	Please, where is the Post Office ?
In jener Strasse, links (rechts).	In that street on the left (right).
Auf Wiedersehen !	Good-bye !

LESSON VI

DECLENSION OF GERMAN NOUNS

We have hitherto dealt in detail only with three types of plurals of nouns:

der Lehrer	die Lehrer
die Nacht	die Nächte
das Dorf	die Dörfer

We are now going to ask the student, in his own interest, to learn by heart (and the sooner the better) the Table of Declensions given on pp. 187–189. If he does this he will have no difficulty in declining (or giving the different forms of) any noun he may come across. Learning these lists will also add to his vocabulary a number of very useful words of which he has need. Some teachers do not advise learning lists by heart, but it is much more important and useful than learning a few poems by heart, and the student should even then constantly refer to the Table and the lists. For instance, suppose he comes across a masculine monosyllable, say, der Kopf, *the head*. *Masculine monosyllables*, says the Table, have their plural in -e (except a few easily learnt by heart in List 5 on page 189) and some have the Umlaut in the plural, while others have not. The list of those which have not is given on page 188, and reference to that (until the whole list is known by heart) will show that der Kopf does not occur there. Therefore der Kopf has the Umlaut in the plural.

Similarly, he will notice that of the *Feminine* nouns, die Mutter and die Tochter only are in Declension 1 (both taking the Umlaut), there are about 30 in Declension 2 (all monosyllables and all taking the Umlaut in the plural), whereas all other feminine nouns (except those in -nis in Declension 2) are in Declension 4. There are *no feminines* in Declension 3, and the student must never forget that *no feminine noun has any ending in the singular*.

It the student has to deal with a *Neuter* monosyllable, he will refer to List 4 on page 189. If it occurs in that list it takes the Umlaut and ends in -er in the plural. If not it is in Declension 2, does not take any Umlaut in the plural and its plural ending is -e.

Notice particularly that there is *always an* -n *in the Dative plural* whether of nouns, articles or adjectives.

The brackets round the (e) in the Dative singular of Declensions 2 and 3 mean that this e is not always added. It is added as a rule only in the case of monosyllables and need not be added even then.

The brackets round the (e) in Declension 4 mean that where the word already ends in -e or in a weak ending (-el, -en, -er) -n only is added.

We give here the full declension of the nouns indicated in the Table:

Declension I

der Laden, shop		der Wagen, cart, car	
der Laden	die Läden	der Wagen	die Wagen
den Laden	die Läden	den Wagen	die Wagen
des Ladens	der Läden	des Wagens	der Wagen
dem Laden	den Läden	dem Wagen	den Wagen

Declension 2

Masculine

der Kopf, head		der Schuh, shoe	
der Kopf	die Köpfe	der Schuh	die Schuhe
den Kopf	die Köpfe	den Schuh	die Schuhe
des Kopfes	der Köpfe	des Schuhes	der Schuhe
dem Kopf(e)	den Köpfen	dem Schuh(e)	den Schuhen

Feminine		Neuter	
die Nacht, night		das Schaf, sheep	
die Nacht	die Nächte	das Schaf	die Schafe
die Nacht	die Nächte	das Schaf	die Schafe
der Nacht	der Nächte	des Schafes	der Schafe
der Nacht	den Nächten	dem Schaf(e)	den Schafen

Declension 3

Neuter		Masculine	
das Glas, glass		der Mann, man	
das Glas	die Gläser	der Mann	die Männer
das Glas	die Gläser	den Mann	die Männer
des Glases	der Gläser	des Mannes	der Männer
dem Glas(e)	den Gläsern	dem Mann(e)	den Männern

Declension 4

Feminine

die Übung, exercise		die Schwester, sister	
die Übung	die Übungen	die Schwester	die Schwestern
die Übung	die Übungen	die Schwester	die Schwestern
der Übung	der Übungen	der Schwester	der Schwestern
der Übung	den Übungen	der Schwester	den Schwestern

Masculine

der Knabe, boy		der Student, student	
der Knabe	die Knaben	der Student	die Studenten
den Knaben	die Knaben	den Studenten	die Studenten
des Knaben	der Knaben	des Studenten	der Studenten
dem Knaben	den Knaben	dem Studenten	den Studenten

The Table of Declensions on pages 187–189 sums up in a nutshell the whole question of German Nouns, and it will be the student's own fault if he continues to be confused and disheartened by German plurals. The more he refers to those pages and the sooner he learns them by heart the better. They apply to 95 per cent. of the nouns in the German language.

Of the other 5 per cent. we may mention here those nouns in -or (from the Latin) with the stress in the syllable *before* the -or in the singular and on the -or in the plural. Such are der Direk'tor, der Dok'tor, der Profes'sor, etc.

der Profes'sor	die Professo'ren
den Profes'sor	die Professo'ren
des Profes'sors	der Professo'ren
dem Profes'sor	den Professo'ren

Finally there are a few modern words of foreign origin that have their plural in -s, such as das Auto, motor-car:

das Auto	die Autos
das Auto	die Autos
des Autos	der Autos
dem Auto	den Autos

It will be seen from the foregoing that the most important parts of a noun's declension are the Genitive singular and the Nominative plural. Constant practice alone will lead to success.

Vocabulary

der Mantel, coat	die Uhr, clock, watch
das Fenster, window	die Taschenuhr,[1] pocket watch
die Tür, door	der Handschuh,[1] glove
der Stock, stick	das Haar, hair
die Socke, sock	das Bein, leg
der Hut, hat	das Licht, light
die Mütze, cap	der Tag, day
der Anzug,[1] suit	der Vogel, bird
der Knopf, button	die Brust, breast, chest
der Strumpf, stocking	der Kragen, collar

[1] Notice that in the case of Compound Nouns it is the final or main part which has the gender and declension. For example, in Anzug, Zug is a masculine monosyllable, An is a prefix. Therefore der Anzug is declined as a masculine monosyllable.

Exercise 23

Give the number (1, 2, 3, or 4) of the Declension, the Genitive singular and the Nominative plural of the nouns given in the preceding Vocabulary. Thus:

| der Mantel | des Mantels | die Mäntel |

LESSON VII

INDEFINITE ARTICLE AND POSSESSIVE ADJECTIVES

In German as in English there are two articles, the definite—which we now know pretty well—and the indefinite. The indefinite article in English is *a* or *an*. In German it is ein or eine. You had better learn it from this table, which you will readily understand by comparing it with the table of the definite article. Obviously ein can have no plural.

	Masc.	Fem.	Neut.	
Nom.	ein	eine	ein	a (an *or* one)
Acc.	einen	eine	ein	a
Gen.	eines	einer	eines	of a
Dat.	einem	einer	einem	to a

You can readily trace a resemblance to the *endings* of the definite article, and this resemblance will make it easy for you to remember the declension.

There are certain other very important words *that go with nouns* and are declined exactly like ein, eine, ein— only they have a plural. These words are:

		Singular.		Plural.
	Masc.	Fem.	Neut.	All genders.
thy	dein	deine	dein	deine
your	{ Ihr	Ihre	Ihr	Ihre
	{ euer	euere	euer	euere
her, their *or* its	ihr	ihre	ihr	ihre

| | Singular. | | | Plural. |
	Masc.	Fem.	Neut.	All genders.
no (*with a noun*)	kein	keine	kein	keine
my	mein	meine	mein	meine
his *or* its	sein	seine	sein	seine
our	unser	unsere	unser	unsere

Observe that the only difference between ihr (her, its or their) and Ihr (your) is the capital letter. The plurals of the above words have the same endings as the plural of der. Thus:

Nom.	die (the)	-e	deine (thy)	ihre (her, their or its)
Acc.	die	-e	deine	ihre
Gen.	der	-er	deiner	ihrer
Dat.	den	-en	deinen	ihren

There are really *three* ways in German of expressing the English word *your*. If we are speaking of one person with whom we are familiar, we say dein as above. If we are speaking of more than one person with whom we are familiar, we use euer (m.), euere (f.), euer (n.), euere (pl.). Then there is the ordinary polite form—which is the form for us—Ihr, Ihre, Ihr, Ihre.

Declension of Proper Nouns

Names of individual persons and places are called proper nouns. In German it is getting more and more unusual to decline proper nouns. Karl (Charles) might be treated as a Kopf noun, but as a matter of fact the only case in which it changes is the Genitive: Karls Buch = Charles' book. This is clearly just the same as in English. But if we want to use the Dative or Accusative of a proper noun we *may* indicate this by the article which shows which case we mean. To Socrates = dem Sokrates. He saw Jason = er sah den Jason. But this is mainly used with classical names, or colloquially.

To express the Possessive case of proper names ending in a hissing consonant the Germans use -ens: Maxens Buch = *Max's book*. However the use of von is preferred: Max's shoes = die Schuhe von Max.

The names of places (countries, towns, etc.) are usually neuter, and take no article. They form their Genitive by von or by the Genitive -s:

Die Hauptstadt von Deutschland (die Hauptstadt Deutschlands) ist Berlin, the capital of Germany is Berlin.

Feminine names of countries (die Schweiz, Switzerland, die Türkei, etc.) *do* require the article:

Die Hauptstadt der Schweiz, the capital of Switzerland.

Notice that we say die Stadt Berlin, die Universität London, not: die Stadt von Berlin, etc.

-er may be added to names of towns to indicate the inhabitant, or to form an adjective:

Die Berliner sagen das nicht, the Berliners do not say that.
In einer Londoner Zeitung, in a London newspaper.
Pilsener Bier, Pilsen Beer.

Vocabulary

das Land	die Nationalität	die Sprache
Frankreich	der Franzose / die Französin	Französisch
England	der Engländer / die Engländerin	Englisch
Schottland	Schotte, Schottin	Schottisch
Irland	Ire, Irin	Irisch
Deutschland	der Deutsche / die Deutsche	Deutsch
Österreich	Österreicher, -in	
Italien	Italiener, -in	Italienisch
Spanien	Spanier, -in	Spanisch
die Vereinigten Staaten	Amerikaner, -in	
die Schweiz	Schweizer, -in	
Holland	Holländer, -in	Holländisch
Belgien	Belgier, -in	Flämisch
Schweden	Schwede, Schwedin	Schwedisch
Russland	Russe, -in	Russisch
die Tschechoslowakei	Tscheche, -in	Tschechisch
Nordamerika	Nordamerikaner, -in	
Südafrika	Südafrikaner	
die Türkei	Türke, -in	Türkisch

in England, in England
nach England, to England
in Berlin, in Berlin
nach Berlin, to Berlin
aus Moskau, from Moscow
der Bolschewist, Bolshevik
der Faschist, Fascist
der Herr, gentleman

die Frau, lady, woman
der Völkerbund, League of Nations
Genf, Geneva
in der Schweiz, in Switzerland
nach der Schweiz, to Switzerland
der Gesandte, ambassador

Exercise 24

Der Gesandte aus Berlin ist jetzt in London. Ich schickte meinen Bruder nach Genf. Es sind keine Äpfel in dem Garten. Unser Haus ist in dieser Strasse. Ein Spanier aus Madrid ist unten. Hast du meine Handschuhe? Er ist der Neffe eines Lehrers in Köln (Cologne). Wo ist deine Uhr? Hier ist sie. Ottos Anzug war in diesem Zimmer. Ist dies Ihr Hut? Wo ist Marie? Ist dies nicht Ihre Armbanduhr (wrist-watch)? Der Neffe ihrer Magd ist tot. Ich reiche meinem Onkel seinen Hut. Unsere Kühe sind in dem Feld. Marie Schmidts (Smith's) Onkel ist in Paris, und Wilhelms Vater ist in der Schweiz. Die Schwester von Fritz ist in dem Laden ihres Onkels.

Exercise 25

Did he not send any (= sent he no) stockings with the shoes? Her dresses are always very good. I often send (= send often) apples and nuts from my garden to my nephews in Germany. We sometimes visit (= visit sometimes) our uncle in Switzerland. Did you send your nephew to Geneva or to Rome (Rom)? Max's shoes are black and Gisela's gloves are brown. Where is your uncle's house? It is in London. Are the rooms of his house very big? He did not send any (= sent no) buttons with her dresses. Have you a Paris newspaper? My uncle hasn't a car. Did you send my brother's books to London? The houses of our city are tall and beautiful.

LESSON VIII

RULES FOR GENDER

In a general way, every noun meaning a male person or animal is masculine, and every noun meaning a female person or animal is feminine. But the endings of words have so much to do with gender that we cannot depend entirely upon the meaning. In what follows we must try to learn something about the *meanings* of endings, as well as their power in determining gender.

Feminine Terminations

1. In English our great feminine ending is -*ess*: actor, actress, etc. In German the corresponding termination is -in: Spieler = a player, Spielerin = a female player. These nouns double the n before adding -en for the plural: thus, the plural of Königin is Königinnen.

2. Most abstract nouns in German are feminine: that is, nouns denoting qualities or abstractions, such as—truth (Wahrheit), science (Wissenschaft), beauty (Schönheit), gratitude (Dankbarkeit), slavery (Sklaverei'), rescue (Rettung), music (Musik'), harmony (Harmonie'). You will observe that all these nouns are derived from simpler words. Wahr means *true*, Wahrheit, the quality of being true; wissen means *to know*, Wissenschaft, the quality of knowing. These words are therefore called derivative words. The most common terminations which are used to form feminine derivative nouns are: -ung (Eng. -*ing*), -heit (Eng. -*hood*), -schaft (Eng. -*ship*), -ei (Eng. -*y*), and -keit (for which we have no English equivalent).

3. The third rule for feminines is of the greatest possible use. All two-syllabled nouns ending in -e, and meaning things without life, are feminine: as die Tasche = the pocket. This rule has few exceptions.

4. The fourth rule is not so important. Most nouns derived from verbs and ending in -d and -t are feminine. Thus: jagen (to hunt) gives die Jagd (the hunting); fahren (to travel) gives die Fahrt (the journey).

Neuter Terminations

1. -chen and -lein are two terminations which make what are called diminutives of the nouns they are attached to. Bach = brook, Bächlein = little brook *or* brooklet; Dorf = a village, Dörfchen = a little village. chen and lein also express endearment, as Väterchen, Mütterchen. These endings make the noun neuter, whatever its gender was before: thus Fräulein, which means a young or unmarried lady (little Frau), is neuter.

2. The -en of the Infinitive must be regarded as a neuter termination when the Infinitive is used as a noun. Thus: das Jagen = hunting, das Trinken = drinking.

Masculine Terminations

1. Most nouns ending in -en (excluding Infinitives and diminutives) are masculine.

2. Two-syllabled nouns ending in -ich, -ig and -ing are masculine.

So far as is consistent with the above rules the following considerations of *meaning* may be applied in determining gender.

Masculine are names of days, months, seasons, stones, winds.

Neuter are names of metals (except der Stahl, steel), countries, cities, villages, islands.

Exercise 26

Keeping in view all that has been said, arrange the following nouns into three classes according as they are masculine, feminine or neuter.   Go down the columns, not across the page.

Fürstin, princess	Blume, flower
Eiche, oak	Kindlein, baby
Honig, honey	Treppe, staircase
Leben, living	Regen, rain
Eselei, stupid conduct	Edelstein, precious stone
Teppich, carpet	Fröhlichkeit, joyfulness
Februar, February	Büchlein, little book
Gold, gold	Melodie', melody
Übersetzung, translation	Eisen, iron
Schlacht, battle	Löwe, lion
Garten, garden	Sonne, sun
Griechenland, Greece	Liebling, darling
Stunde, hour	Väterchen, little father
Jüngling, youngster	Dummheit, stupidity
Reinheit, purity	Helgoland, Heligoland
Paris, Paris	Käfig, cage
Freundschaft, friendship	Tanzen, dancing
Diamant', diamond	Monat, month
Schrift, writing	Pferdchen, little horse
Poesie', poetry	Kuchen, cake
Rauchen, smoking	Union, union
Freitag, Friday	Blümchen, little flower
Frau, wife	

LESSON IX

NON-PERSONAL ELEMENT IN VERBS

Not every part of a verb has person.   We can say *I* did it, or *you* did it, or *they* did it.   But we cannot use any of these pronouns with *done*.   We cannot say I *done* it, or you *done* it, or they *done* it.   It is true we can say I (or you or they) *have* done it.   But here the personal pronouns do not belong to the *done* but to the *have*.   In other words, *have* is a personal part of the verb; *done* is a non-personal.   *Done* is called the Past Principle, and can never be used with a personal pronoun without the help of another verb like *have* or *was*.   It is for this reason that certain verbs—such as *to have* and *to be*—are called auxiliary or helping verbs.

In English the most common ending for the Past Participle is *-ed*—he has play-ed, work-ed, arrang-ed, borrow-ed, etc. Here are some examples of English and German Past Participles:

Present Tense	loves	liebt	plays	spielt	says	sagt
Past Tense	loved	liebte	played	spielte	said	sagte
Past Participle	loved	geliebt	played	gespielt	said	gesagt

From this we may infer that most German Past Participles begin with ge and end with t.

Once we know the Past Participle of a verb, we can use it to make a new Past tense by the help of *have*. Thus: er hat gesagt = *he has said*, or simply *he said*. This tense is called the *Perfect*, because the action is now complete. Again we may say, er hatte gesagt = he *had* said. This is called the *Pluperfect* tense, because the action was completed at some time now past.

Perfect of lieben

Singular

1.	ich habe geliebt	I have loved
2.	du hast geliebt	thou hast loved
3.	er hat geliebt	he has loved

Plural

1.	wir haben geliebt	we have loved
2.	{Sie haben (ihr habt)} geliebt	you have loved
3.	sie haben geliebt	they have loved

Here we see that geliebt remains unchanged. Everything depends upon the personal verb haben. Geliebt, in fact, is hardly a verb at all: it is really a sort of adjective. The Germans throw the Past Participle always away to the very end of the sentence. We say, *he has said the word*. The Germans say, *he has the word said*: er hat das Wort gesagt. *The child had loved the mother of his friend* = Das Kind hatte die Mutter seines Freundes geliebt.

The Infinitive is another non-personal part of the verb, and is treated in the same unceremonious way by the Germans, who put it at the very end. *I will not say that word* = Ich will jenes Wort nicht sagen. Observe that *say* is here Infinitive, though the *to* is omitted, just as the zu is omitted before sagen. The full Infinitive in German is zu sagen, but the zu is omitted with auxiliaries, as here. Examples will be given later in the Course of the retention of this zu.

In English all Past Participles do not end in *ed*, though that is the regular ending. The following are Past Participles: *done, been, drunk, slept, arisen*. In the same way all German Past Participles do not begin with ge and end with t, though that is the regular thing. In the following list of verbs the first nine are regular, the last six irregular:

Pres. Infin.	Past Tense	Past Part.	Meaning
kaufen	kaufte	gekauft	to buy
suchen	suchte	gesucht	to seek
töten	tötete	getötet	to kill
warten	wartete	gewartet	to wait
bauen	baute	gebaut	to build
antworten	antwortete	geantwortet	to answer
wählen	wählte	gewählt	to choose
retten	rettete	gerettet	to save
arbeiten	arbeitete	gearbeitet	to work
brennen	brannte	gebrannt [1]	to burn
denken	dachte	gedacht	to think
bringen	brachte	gebracht	to bring
senden	sandte	gesandt	to send
nennen	nannte	genannt	to name
kennen	kannte	gekannt	to know [2]

[1] When *to burn* means *to burn up* or *consume*, it is verbrennen, verbrannte, verbrannt.

[2] When *to know* means to recognise through the five senses.

You will observe that when the stem of a regular verb ends in -d or -t, an extra e is inserted in the Past and Past Participle. This is for the sake of the sound; your ear will keep you right in this matter.

The Use of the Perfect

This tense is used to express an action that has been going on and is still continuing, or a finished action of recent occurrence, or vaguely in the past. For example:

> Ich habe meine Handschuhe gesucht. I have been looking for my gloves.
> Er hat mir nicht geantwortet. He did not answer me.
> Der Mönch Schwartz hat das Schiesspulver entdeckt. The monk Schwartz discovered gunpowder.

Vocabulary

die See, sea	die Frau, woman, wife
der Soldat, soldier	das Land, country
das Klavier, piano	Klavier spielen, to play the piano
die Musik, music	
das Radio, wireless	Radio hören, to listen to the wireless
das Grammophon, gramophone	
der Stuhl, chair	gern haben, to like (= have willingly)
der Teppich, carpet	
die Zigarre, cigar	gern hören, to like (listening to)
die Zigarette, cigarette	
die Pfeife, pipe	baden, to bathe, swim
der Schnee, snow	gern rauchen, to like smoking
die Annonce, advertisement	zu Weihnachten, at Christmas
der Hund, dog	auf, on (top of) (with Dat.)
im Winter, in winter	an, on (side of), to (with Acc.)
im Sommer, in summer	der Wald, wood
der Stock, stick	

Exercise 27

Hast du dem Neffen des Bäckers das Buch des Lehrers geschickt? Ich habe die Löwen in dem Walde gehört. Hat die Magd die Äpfel nicht gekocht? Mein Bruder hat meinem Vater telephoniert. Ich habe meinem Onkel seinen Stock gereicht. Dieses Mädchen hat

Klavier gespielt. Rauchen Sie gerne (or gern) Zigaretten? Nein, ich rauche immer eine Pfeife. Zu Weihnachten schicken wir unserem Bruder Äpfel, Nüsse, Bücher und Zigaretten. Hören Sie gern Musik an dem Radio? Wir haben in einem Hause in jenem Dorfe gewohnt. Die Soldaten haben die Hauptstadt des Landes verbrannt. Meine Schwester hat die Annonce in der Zeitung gesucht. Wir haben unseren Hund Mops genannt. Welches Buch hat deine Schwester gewählt? Die Soldaten haben keine Frauen und Kinder getötet. Im Sommer haben wir oft in der See gebadet. Die Schüler haben im Winter mit dem Schnee gespielt. Ich habe Hunde nicht gern.

Exercise 28

Have you (du) been dreaming? No, I have been drawing that house. Which book is on your chair? This carpet is very old. I like listening to the wireless. Does your father like smoking? Yes, he has always smoked cigars. I often smoke (= smoke often) cigars at Christmas. In the summer we have (= have we) visited our uncle in Switzerland. Have you sent those newspapers to Geneva? The baker and his wife have named their child Margarete. The tailor has not made the dress. Otto's sister has been playing the piano, and my brothers have been listening to the music on the wireless. Has the tailor brought the dress? In which shop did you buy (Perfect tense) that hat? Do you like bathing in the sea? I like listening to the gramophone.

LESSON X

PERSONAL PRONOUNS

He, she and *it* are easily used in English. But in German they require careful watching. We must not think of sex at all, but only of the gender of the noun to which these little words apply. Talking of the town in German, we must not say it *is fine*, but she *is fine*, since Stadt is feminine: sie ist schön. So of a table we must say he *is round*: er ist rund. Of a maiden (Mädchen) we say it *is clever*: es ist geschickt; but we may also say sie ist geschickt. You must therefore never use *he* or *she* or *it* without looking carefully at the gender of the noun referred to.

In English we have these words declined:

	Singular			Plural
	Masc.	Fem.	Neut.	All Genders
Nom.	he	she	it	they
Acc.	him	her	it	them

Corresponding to these we have the German forms:

	Singular		Plural
	Masc.	Fem.	Masc. and Fem.
Nom.	er	sie	sie
Acc.	ihn	sie	sie
Dat.	ihm	ihr	ihnen

I saw him, but not her.   Ich sah ihn, aber nicht sie.

I have this book from him.   Ich habe dieses Buch von ihm.

We have sent her a present.   Wir haben ihr ein Geschenk gesandt.

Pay careful attention to what we have said about *it*. The fact is that the English *it* can be put into German in three different ways according to what *it* refers to. If *it* refers to a table (Tisch), it is masculine and is rendered er; if *it* refers to a street (Strasse), it is feminine and is represented by sie; if *it* refers to a book (Buch), it is neuter and is rendered by es. All these are Nominative: if *it* is in the Accusative, it is ihn (m.), or sie (f.), or es (n.). You will learn the use of these words much better from observing the following examples:

Where is my pen?   I saw it in your room.   Wo ist meine Feder?   Ich sah sie in Ihrem Zimmer.

She has brought my shoe : where is it ? Sie hat meinen
   Schuh gebracht : wo ist er ?
Where is the dog ? We have sent it to him. Wo ist der
   Hund ? Wir haben ihn ihm gesandt.
It was my house, but the soldiers have burned it. Es war
   mein Haus, aber die Soldaten haben es verbrannt.

The *pronoun as an object*, whether direct (Accusative)
or indirect (Dative), *precedes a noun object, i.e.* it follows
the verb. *Of two pronoun objects*, the *direct* (Accusative) *precedes the indirect* (Dative), that is, the opposite
order to two noun objects. *E.g.*:

   Ich schicke es dem Bäcker. I send it to the baker.
   Ich schicke es ihm. I send it to him.

Vocabulary

der Baum, tree	hell, bright
der Wind, wind	stark, strong
die Sonne, sun	schwach, weak
der Mond, moon	teuer, dear
der Stern, star	billig, cheap
der Rasen, lawn	heiss, hot
das Wetter, weather	warm, warm
die Wolke, cloud	kalt, cold
der Regen, rain	jung, young
der Teich, pond	wer ? who ?
der Nebel, fog	wen ? whom ? (Acc.)
der Fluss, river	wem ? to whom ? (Dat.)
das Wasser, water	wann ? when ?
kaum, scarcely	niemals, never
nur, only	nichts, nothing
gestern, yesterday	

Exercise 29

Ich habe nichts gehört. Gestern war die Sonne ganz
warm. Wem hast du den Weihnachtsbaum (Christ-
mas-) geschickt ? Ich habe ihn meinem Neffen geschickt.
Jene Wolken sind gross und schwarz, sie bringen Regen.
Das Wetter ist sehr kalt, und es (= there) ist Nebel auf
dem Fluss. Wann haben Sie diesen Anzug gekauft ?

Ich habe ihn gestern in jenem Laden gekauft. War er billig oder teuer? Er war ganz billig. Die Sterne sind klein, aber der Mond ist gross. Haben Sie Ihrer Schwester die Armbanduhr geschickt? Ja, ich habe sie ihr gestern geschickt. Hat dein Vater den Kindern den Weihnachtsbaum geschickt? Ja, er hat ihn ihnen gestern geschickt. Es sind drei Hunde auf dem Rasen; mein Neffe spielt mit ihnen.

Exercise 30

The sun was not very bright yesterday. When did you answer? There were seven or eight sailors on the river. This river is very long. We scarcely heard (= heard scarcely) the children's song. Whom did you visit in Switzerland? These motor-cars are almost too cheap. To whom did you telephone yesterday? Here is your hat. Where did you buy it? I am sending it (*i.e.* the hat) to my brother. The children have been looking for the apples. I have handed them to them. We never have (= have never) fog in this country. Who answered him? Have you 'phoned to her? Was the wind very strong yesterday? The sky was blue and the clouds were small and white. The water in the pond was too cold yesterday. We did not bathe. I have said nothing to him. She only smiled (= smiled only). We scarcely heard them.

LESSON XI

STRONG VERBS

Taking the three parts of the verb—the Infinitive, the Imperfect, and the Past Participle—we find that most of the verbs with which we have dealt up till now have had the form lieben, liebte, geliebt; spielen, spielte, gespielt. This is what is known as the *Weak* Conjugation, or the *New* Conjugation. The best way to learn the difference between the New and the Old Conjugation is to examine the following list of verbs, and see how they differ from the verbs we have been dealing with:

Some Verbs of the Strong or Old Conjugation

Infinitive	Imperfect	Past Part.	Meaning
schlagen	schlug	geschlagen	to strike
geben	gab	gegeben	to give
heissen	hiess	geheissen	to be called
nehmen	nahm	genommen	to take
reiten	ritt	geritten	to ride
laufen	lief	gelaufen	to run
kommen	kam	gekommen	to come
singen	sang	gesungen	to sing
essen	ass	gegessen	to eat (of people)
fressen	frass	gefressen	to eat (of animals)
spinnen	spann	gesponnen	to spin
trinken	trank	getrunken	to drink
fliegen	flog	geflogen	to fly
sehen	sah	gesehen	to see
stehen	stand	gestanden	to stand
brechen	brach	gebrochen	to break
beginnen	begann	begonnen	to begin
sprechen	sprach	gesprochen	to speak
fahren	fuhr	gefahren	to drive

Read over the above list five or six times, so as to impress the general run of the sound upon the ear.

On careful examination, you will note several points in which all those verbs agree with each other, and differ from the lieben, liebte, geliebt conjugation.

1. The Past Participles *all end in* -en, not in t.

2. The Imperfect has *no ending at all*, instead of in te.

3. The *vowel of the Imperfect is always different* from the vowel of the Infinitive.

You will note that some of the verbs have three different vowel sounds, others have only two. When there are only two sounds, sometimes it is the Infinitive and sometimes the Imperfect which is the same as the Past Participle.

As a test at this stage, arrange the above nineteen verbs in three classes: (1) Those having three different vowel sounds; (2) those in which the Infinitive and Past Participle have the same vowel; and (3) those in which the Imperfect and the Past Participle have the same vowel.

Observe now the full conjugation of the Imperfect, and note how it differs from the liebte type:

Imperfect of Certain Strong or Old Verbs

1.	ich	schlug	lief	ass	sah	kam
2.	du	schlugst	liefst	assest	sahst	kamst
3.	er	schlug	lief	ass	sah	kam
1.	wir	schlugen	liefen	assen	sahen	kamen
2.	{Sie	schlugen	liefen	assen	sahen	kamen
	{ihr	schlugt	lieft	asst	saht	kamt
3.	sie	schlugen	liefen	assen	sahen	kamen

Clearly the most striking difference is *the total absence of any termination in both first and third person singular*. You cannot help noting how exceedingly regular the conjugation is. Given the first person singular you cannot fail to complete the whole.

With the Present tense of old or strong verbs this regularity is not present. The plural of the Present tense is all right: it is, indeed, simply the Infinitive with the usual pronouns placed before it. Even in the singular the first person always has the same vowel as the Infinitive. It is the second and third persons singular that give trouble by sometimes changing their vowel sounds. You will understand this better by examining carefully the following:

Present of Certain Strong or Old Verbs

1.	ich	schlage	laufe	esse	sehe	komme
2.	du	schlägst	läufst	isst	siehst	kommst
3.	er	schlägt	läuft	isst	sieht	kommt
1.	wir	schlagen	laufen	essen	sehen	kommen
2.	{Sie	schlagen	laufen	essen	sehen	kommen
	{ihr	schlagt	lauft	esst	seht	kommt
3.	sie	schlagen	laufen	essen	sehen	kommen

The change of vowel in the 2nd and 3rd person does not always take place, as we find from kommen, although the verb stossen, *to push*, has du stöss(es)t, er stösst. The main changes are:

      (i) a is changed into ä
      (ii) au   ,,   ,,   äu
      (iii) e (long) is changed into ie
      (iv) e (short)   ,,   ,,   i

Keeping in view all that has been said, write out, as above, the Present and the Imperfect of the following six verbs:

bitten	bat	gebeten	to beg *or* ask
befehlen	befahl	befohlen	to command
sterben	starb	gestorben	to die
fahren	fuhr	gefahren	to drive
geben	gab	gegeben	to give
nehmen	nahm	genommen	to take

Notice that geben (although e long) has gibst, gibt, and nehmen has nimmst, nimmt in the Present tense. The form giebst, giebt is old-fashioned.

[See Appendix B, pp. 190–195.]

Vocabulary

das Pferd, horse	das Heu, hay
der Esel, donkey	das Gras, grass
die Katze, cat	der Tee, tea
das Schwein, pig	der Zucker, sugar
die Biene, bee	die Blume, flower
die Wespe, wasp	das Gewebe, web
die Spinne, spider	melken, to milk
der Knecht, farm-hand	füttern, to feed
der Bauernhof, farm	pflügen, to plough
der Bauer, farmer	säen, to sow
die Bäuerin, farmer's wife	bellen, to bark
der Stall, stable	miauen, to mew
die Peitsche, whip	summen, to buzz
das Brot, bread	iahen, to bray
der Honig, honey	grunzen, to grunt
die Arbeit, work	im Frühling, in spring
von . . . zu, from . . . to	im Herbst, in the autumn
laut, loud, loudly	was? what?

Exercise 31

Die Spinne war gross und dick; sie spann ein Gewebe.
Die Biene summte; sie flog von Blume zu Blume und
suchte Honig. Was frisst die Wespe? Sie frisst Zucker.
Die Esel iahten, die Schweine grunzten, die Hunde
bellten und die Katzen miauten. Der Knecht ritt auf
einem Pferd. Er fütterte die Ochsen, die Schafe und die
Kühe. Sein Hund lief mit ihm. Er bellte zu laut. Der
Bauer schlug ihn mit seiner Peitsche. Die Bäuerin
melkte (or molk) die Kühe in dem Stall. Es sind acht
oder neun Knechte auf dem Bauernhof. Sie arbeiten
immer. Im Herbst pflügen sie die Felder. Im Frühling
säen sie. Der Bauer hiess Herr Braun. Er stand auf
(got up) und begann seine Arbeit. Er fuhr in seinem
Wagen zu dem Feld. Was ass er? Er ass Brot und
trank Tee mit Zucker. Seine Kinder sangen Lieder.
Er gab ihnen Äpfel und Nüsse.

Exercise 32

The farmer drove to the fields. He took his children.
They liked to see (= saw willingly) the cows, sheep
and horses in the fields. The boy was called Karl.
He liked to ride on a donkey. He gave it (= him) hay.
The donkey likes eating sugar.

Karl's dog is in the garden. It is big and strong.
It breaks the flowers. Karl runs after him and strikes
him with his whip. The dog barks loudly. The sun
is warm and bright. The bees are buzzing and flying
from flower to flower. They like honey. Do you like
honey? Karl does not see the spider. It is big and fat.
It has spun a web. Do you like spiders?

Have you already begun your work? I have broken [1]
my watch. Has your uncle given his nephew a watch?
Have you (du) drunk your tea? Yes, and I have already
eaten my bread and honey.

[1] Use zerbrechen.

LESSON XII

PREPOSITIONS AND WERDEN

With Accusative or Dative

We have had some prepositions that govern the dative and some that govern the accusative. But now we must have some that sometimes govern the dative and sometimes the accusative. There are nine of them:

an, at (with dat.)	neben, besides, near
an, to (with acc.)	über, over or across
auf, on, upon	vor, before, in front of
hinter, behind	unter, under or among
in, in or at (with dat.)	zwischen, between
in, into (with acc.)	

The meaning tells us when to use the accusative, when the dative. If there is any *motion towards* anything implied, then the accusative is used; if no such motion is implied, the dative.

Er ist auf dem Berge.	He is on the mountain.
Er läuft auf dem Berge.	He runs on the mountain.
Er läuft auf den Berg.	He runs to the mountain.
Er ging in das Haus.	He went into the house.
Er war in dem Hause.	He was in the house.
Sie sass auf dem Stuhl.	She sat on the chair.
Sie sprang auf den Stuhl.	She sprang upon the chair.

With Dative only

To keep matters clear we had better repeat the more common prepositions that govern only the dative:

aus, out	samt } along with
bei, by, at, with, near	nebst } along with
gegenüber, opposite	seit, since
mit, with	von, of
nach, after	zu, to

Gegenüber often follows the noun.

C

With Accusative only

durch, through	ohne, without
für, for	um, about, round
gegen, against	wider, against

With Genitive only

anstatt *or* statt, instead of	trotz, in spite of
diesseits, on this side of	während, during
jenseits, on that side of	wegen, on account of
mittels, by means of	

Observe that all except während have the English equivalent ending in *of*. This is a good way of remembering which case these prepositions govern.

Contraction of Preposition and Article

Just as we contract *do not* into *don't*, so the Germans are fond of contracting their prepositions and their articles into one word. Thus:

an dem becomes am	bei dem becomes beim
an das „ ans	von dem „ vom
auf das „ aufs	(vor das „ vors)
in dem „ im	zu dem „ zum
in das „ ins	zu der „ zur

Special Notes on the Translation of *To*

(i) When *to* shows the receiver of an object, use the single dative without preposition (see also Lesson XXIV):

Er gab seiner Schwester das Buch. He gave the book to his sister.
Er schickte Resi ein Buch. He sent a book to Resi.

(ii) Indicating motion towards a person, zu:

Er kam zu seiner Mutter. He came to his mother.

(iii) Motion towards a large object or place (not a proper name), zu :

Er lief zu dem Bauernhof. He ran to the farm.
N.B. From . . . to = von . . . zu.

(iv) Motion towards smaller objects, and sending letters to persons, *an*:

> Er ging an das Fenster, an den Spiegel, an die Tür. He went to the window (mirror, door).
>
> Ich schrieb einen Brief an meine Mutter. I wrote a letter to my mother.

—although one would not usually use *an* with a pronoun in this case, but the dative of the pronoun:

> Ich schrieb ihr einen Brief.

(v) *To* before a place (proper name), *nach*:

> Wir fuhren nach Spanien, nach Köln. We went to Spain, to Cologne.

(vi) *To* = *auf* in the following cases:

> Auf die Post, auf den Markt, auf die Universität, auf die Polizei, auf die Bank, to the post-office (the market, university, police-station, bank).
>
> N.B. To (into) the country, auf das Land. To the seaside, an die See.

(vii) When *into* as well as *to* is implied, *in*:

> Er geht in die Schule, in die Kirche, in die Stadt, ins Kino, ins Theater. He is going to school, to church, to the town, cinema, theatre.

(viii) To talk *to*, *sprechen mit*:

> Ich sprach mit dem Bürgermeister. I was talking to the mayor.

(ix) *To* = in order to, *um . . . zu* (+ Infinitive):

> Er ging aus, um die Pferde zu füttern. He went out to feed the horses.

(x) Note the following indefinite directions:

> Nach rechts (links), to the right, to the left.
> Von oben nach unten, from top to bottom.
> Von hinten nach vorn, from back to front.

Vocabulary

die Tür, door	das Café (—s, —s),[2] café
das Tor, gate	beim Krämer, at the grocer's
die Mauer, wall [1]	das Krankenhaus, hospital
das Restaurant, restaurant	der Verkehr, traffic
der Park, park	die Telephonzelle, telephone-box
der Fussgänger, pedestrian	
das Warenhaus, big stores	der Wolkenkratzer, "sky-scraper"
die Strasse, street	
die Strassenlampe, street-lamp	*liegen, to lie, be situated
der Brief, letter	kaufen, to buy
der Polizist, policeman	verkaufen, to sell
die Strassenecke, street-corner	prachtvoll, magnificent
die Brücke, bridge	gefährlich, dangerous
das Rathaus, Town Hall	führen, to lead, drive, take
das Schaufenster, shop-window	*wiegen, to weigh
der Marktplatz, market-place	verlangen, to ask for
der Briefkasten, letter-box	bewundern, to admire
das Gebäude, building	bezahlen, to pay (for)
*schliessen, to shut	nach Hause * gehen, to go home
angestellt, employed	zu Hause * sein, to be at home

* From now on strong verbs are marked with an asterisk (*), and their principal parts are to be found in the Appendix, pp. 190–195.

A Note on the English *to put*

Some care must be exercised in translating *to put*. Note the following:

(i) In a general way, setzen.
(ii) To put a thing *standing up* (as a vase), stellen.
(iii) To put a thing *lying down* (as a book), legen.
(iv) To put away out of sight, as in a drawer, pocket, etc., stecken.
(v) To put = to add (as salt in potatoes, etc.), * tun (literally *to do*).

Exercise 33

Unsere Bank liegt zwischen der Post und der Marien-kirche.[3] Ich habe meinem Bruder von einer Telephon-

---

[1] die Wand is the surface, die Mauer the thickness.
[2] Gen. sing. and Nom. pl.
[3] die Marienkirche, St. Mary's Church.

zelle telephoniert. Es sind viele Wolkenkratzer in unserer Stadt. Das Gebäude des Völkerbundes war in Genf, in der Schweiz. Es waren Bolschewisten in Russland und Faschisten in Italien und Deutschland. Die Soldaten sind vor dem Tore der Stadt. Es sind Italiener und Spanier.

Ich ging ins Restaurant. Ich habe gegessen und bezahlt. Ich kam aus dem Restaurant und ging zum Marktplatz. Ich ging ins Kino. Das Kino war gross und schön, aber es war kein Wolkenkratzer. Im Kino waren Männer, Frauen und Kinder. Ich gehe oft ins Theater. Gehen Sie gern ins Theater? Ich sah ein Krankenhaus neben dem Park. Gegenüber dem Warenhaus (dem Warenhaus gegenüber) war das Rathaus. Dieses Gebäude ist prachtvoll. Ich sagte zu einem Polizisten: "Wo ist ein Briefkasten?" Er antwortete: "Dort an der Strassenecke." Ich steckte einen Brief in den Briefkasten. Mein Bruder ist bei einem Krämer angestellt. Er verkauft Zucker, Tee usw.[1] Hinter dem Rathaus war die Paulskirche.[2] Ich ging unter eine Brücke. Diese Brücke war sehr hoch. Über die Brücke fahren Autos und Pferde. Der Verkehr ist sehr gefährlich für die Fussgänger.

Exercise 34

I put my book on a chair. The weather was fairly warm. I ran out of the room. I went through the door and into [3] the street. It was dark but the street was quite bright on account of (because of, owing to) the street-lamps. There were eight motor-cars and three horses in the street. I went with my dog round the town. My dog ran between the motor-cars. I went into a telephone box and 'phoned to my sister. She is employed

---

[1] usw. = und so weiter, and so on, *or* etc.
[2] die Paulskirche, St. Paul's Church.
[3] Of persons, vehicles, etc. *auf*, otherwise *in* before *Strasse*.

in a hospital near St. Paul's Church. I live with my brother opposite the Town Hall. We went to the right and came to a bridge. It was fairly low. We looked down [1] on to the traffic. The traffic since the war is very dangerous. My uncle was in that car. He was driving to the Market Place. He has a shop there. He often drives (= drives often) over this bridge. Our village lay on the other side of the river. In front of our house stood a lamp-post (street-lamp). We went into a restaurant to eat. After the meal [2] I went home without my dog, but I saw him at home, in front of the door.

There is a very useful little verb called werden, which means to *become* or to *get*, in the sense of *getting* angry or *getting* grey. The Present Indicative goes quite easily:

Present of werden

Singular	Plural
1. ich werde	wir werden
2. du wirst	{ Sie werden { ihr werdet
3. er wird	sie werden

The great use of this verb is to form the Future of all other verbs. To make the Future all we have to do is to add the Infinitive of the verb we want to the proper part of werden :

I shall buy.	Ich werde kaufen.
You will speak.	Sie werden sprechen.
The boy will learn.	Der Knabe wird lernen.
The horse will run.	Das Pferd wird laufen.

If we want to have what is called the *Future Perfect*— *i.e.* to express something that will be completely done at some future time—we have to use haben along with the Past Participle of the required verb:

I shall have bought.	Ich werde gekauft haben.
You will have spoken.	Sie werden gesprochen haben.
The boy will have learnt.	Der Knabe wird gelernt haben.

---

[1] To look down on, sehen auf (*acc.*).   [2] The meal, das Essen.

The Perfect tense of haben is formed in the ordinary way:

> Ich habe viele Äpfel von diesem Baum gehabt.   I have had many apples from this tree.

But the Perfect tense of sein is formed with the Present tense of sein + Past Participle:

> ich bin gewesen, I have been (*literally :* I am been).
> du bist gewesen, you have been.
> er ist gewesen, he has been, etc.

Vocabulary

morgen, to-morrow	um halb vier, at half past three
morgen früh, tomorrow morning	am Abend, in the evening
nächste Woche, next week	am Nachmittag, in the after-
nächsten Sonntag, next Sunday	noon
„ Montag, „ Monday	abends, in the evening(s)
„ Dienstag, „ Tuesday	morgens, in the morning(s)
„ Mittwoch „ Wednes-	nachmittags, in the after-
day	noon(s)
„ Donnerstag, next	bald, soon
Thursday	früh, early
„ Freitag, next Friday	spät, late
„ Samstag, „ Saturday	schnell, quickly
heute, to-day	eines Tages, one day
heute morgen, this morning	nächstes Jahr, next year
heute nachmittag, this afternoon	der Bahnhof, station (railway)
heute abend, this evening	die U-bahn (die Untergrund-
der Freund, friend	bahn), Underground (rail-
das Flugzeug, aeroplane	way)
um zwei Uhr, at 2 o'clock	

Exercise 35

Morgen werde ich zum Marktplatz gehen.   Was werden Sie dort tun?   Ich werde zwei drei [1] Pferde kaufen. Sind sie billig oder teuer?   Sie sind dieses Jahr ziemlich teuer.   Werden Sie mit [2] dem Auto fahren?   Heute ist das Wetter sehr kalt.   Wir werden bald Schnee haben.

---

[1] zwei drei = two *or* three.
[2] To travel *by* a vehicle, fahren mit.

Was wird dein Onkel nächsten Dienstag tun? Er wird nach Lissabon [1] fliegen. Heute nachmittag werden wir ins Kino gehen. Gehen Sie gern ins Kino? Meine Brüder werden eines Tages nach Köln fliegen. Heute abend wird meine Schwester Klavier spielen, und Elses Bruder wird Lieder singen. Ich werde die Musik am Radio hören. Ich höre gerne Radio.

Gestern habe ich einen Brief von meinem Onkel gehabt. Zu Weihnachten wird er meinem Vater einen Weihnachtsbaum schicken. Er ist letzte Woche in Frankreich gewesen. Das Wetter war sehr kalt dort. Sie haben Nebel und Regen gehabt. Ich bin niemals in Frankreich gewesen. Warst du schon in Paris? [2]

Exercise 36

Next Friday I shall travel to Germany. Will you go by car to London? No, I shall travel by the Underground (by " tube "). What will you do in Germany? I shall visit one or two friends. Will you go (= travel) by air (= with the aeroplane)? No, I don't like travelling by air. Have you ever been to Germany? [2] Yes, I was there last year (= last year ,there). To which station will you go? To Liverpool Street. [3] The weather has not been very warm.

LESSON XIII

DECLENSION OF ADJECTIVES

Words which indicate qualities in connection with nouns and pronouns are called adjectives. We have already used several of them, such as gut, schlecht, böse, arm, jung. But if you care to look back over your exercises you will find that all the adjectives we have

[1] Lisbon.
[2] Were you already in = have you ever been to ?
[3] Do not translate.

used have been used along with some part of the verb *to be*. We have never used an adjective *before* a noun. We have said often something like *the man is good*: we have never spoken of *the good man*.

The first way (the man is good) is called the *predicative* use of the adjective; the second (the good man) is called the *attributive* use of the adjective. In English there is no difference in the form of the word *good*: it is exactly the same in both cases. In German there is a very important difference. In the predicative use the adjective does not change at all. If you look back at all the exercises and examples you will not find any change in any adjective.[1]

But in the attributive use the adjective must be declined so as to agree with its noun in both number and gender. We say, der Mann ist gut; ein Mädchen ist gut; die Stadt ist gut; die Knaben sind gut: using the same word gut in every case. But we must say, ein guter Mann; ein gutes Mädchen; die gute Stadt; die guten Knaben.

The changes that the attributive adjective undergoes are different according to whether an article is or is not used with it. There are three cases:

I. WHEN THE ADJECTIVE IS USED WITHOUT ANY ARTICLE. Here the terminations of the adjective are merely the terminations of the definite article as they are changed in the demonstratives like dieser.

	Singular			Plural
	Masc.	Fem.	Neut.	All Genders
Nom.	-er	-e	-es	-e
Acc.	-en	-e	-es	-e
Gen.	(-es) -en	-er	(-es) -en	-er
Dat.	-em	-er	-em	-en

The -en in the two genitives is put in to show that now for the sake of sound en is preferred to es. Guten

---

[1] We are not speaking here of demonstratives like dieser, or possessives like mein.

Brotes seems to sound better than gutes Brotes in the ears of a German.

2. WHEN THE ADJECTIVE IS USED WITH THE DEFINITE ARTICLE. Here we have a very pretty form, which is easily remembered as a mental picture of five e's among a crowd of en's.

	Singular			Plural
	Masc.	Fem.	Neut.	All Genders
Nom.	-e	-e	-e	-en
Acc.	-en	-e	-e	-en
Gen.	-en	-en	-en	-en
Dat.	-en	-en	-en	-en

The above form is also used after four words that we already know: dieser, jener, welcher, and some new ones: mancher = many a, derselbe (or der nämliche) = the same, and der andere = the other.

3. WHEN THE ADJECTIVE IS USED WITH THE IN-DEFINITE ARTICLE. This is not quite so regular as No. 2, but *all the en's remain unchanged.*

	Singular			Plural
	Masc.	Fem.	Neut.	All Genders
Nom.	-er	-e	-es	-en
Acc.	-en	-e	-es	-en
Gen.	-en	-en	-en	-en
Dat.	-en	-en	-en	-en

The same form is used with the words: mein, dein, sein, kein, ihr, Ihr, euer, unser.

Notice that after any of the determinative words mentioned (der, mein, kein, welcher, etc.) there is *always* -en *in the Genitive and Dative and always in the Plural,* and if the determinative word ends in -en, then the adjective also ends in -en (masculine singular accusative).

Vocabulary

lustig, jolly, merry	unbequem, uncomfortable
traurig, sad	eng, narrow
hübsch, pretty	breit, broad
hässlich, ugly	stumm, dumb

rein, clean
schmutzig, dirty
*tragen, to wear, carry
klug, clever, intelligent
dumm, silly, stupid
blind, blind
taub, deaf
bequem, comfortable

der Grossvater, grandfather
die Grossmutter, grandmother
der Vetter (—s, —n), (boy) cousin
die Kusine, (girl) cousin
die Tante, aunt
das Taschentuch, handkerchief

Exercise 37

Give the Nominative Singular, Genitive Singular and Nominative Plural of the following:

einem grossen Baum, einer kleinen Blume, keinem blinden Manne, einem kleinen Mädchen, welcher breiten Strasse, den starken Hunden, der klugen Kusine, dem tauben Vetter, den hässlichen alten Frauen, kaltem Winde, demselben schmutzigen Jungen.

Exercise 38

Das traurige Mädchen weint immer. Deutsche Bücher sind nicht immer schwer. Die kleine Tochter des dicken Bäckers gab dem klugen Neffen des alten Schneiders einen Brief. Ein kluger Junge lernt schnell. Die kleinen Kinder spielten auf dem weichen Gras. Sie spielen nicht gern auf der harten Strasse. Der alte Grossvater ist blind, und seine alte Frau ist sehr taub. Das hübsche Mädchen trägt ein neues Kleid mit roten Knöpfen. Karl hat ein reines Taschentuch in der Tasche seines braunen Anzugs. Der Verkehr ist in diesen engen Strassen sehr gefährlich. Zwei blinde Männer gingen mit ihrem weissen Hunde über die breite Strasse. Hübsche Mädchen sind nicht immer dumm.

Exercise 39

Little boys are nearly always dirty. I shall visit an old friend in Geneva. Blind men are not always sad. The narrow streets of the old city were very dark. I do not like this uncomfortable old chair. My beautiful cousin sang French, Spanish and German songs. I like listening to good music on the wireless. The Italian ambassador came to London yesterday (= yesterday to London). Marie's cousin was wearing a green dress and a white hat. Which German book have you chosen?

LESSON XIV

RELATIVE PRONOUNS

Certain pronouns, called relative pronouns, both relate to nouns or pronouns previously mentioned in a sentence, and join clauses together. *The knight who sent it is dead.* Here *who* is a relative pronoun, referring back to *knight*, and at the same time joining the clause *the knight is dead* to the clause *who sent it.* Some people say that *who* here is equal to *and he.*

There are two ways of translating the relative pronouns into German.

The shorter and more frequently used form of the German relative is nothing but the definite article with the genitive singular, the genitive and dative plural changed somewhat.

	Masc.		Fem.	Neut.		Plural All Genders
Nom.	der	who	die	das	which *or* that	die
Acc.	den	whom	die	das	which *or* that	die
Gen.	dessen	whose	deren	dessen	of which	deren
Dat.	dem	to whom	der	dem	to which	denen

Note that the dative plural of the relative is denen, to show that it *is* plural. With the article, den is enough, for the noun shows whether it is singular or plural.

	Masc.		Fem.	Neut.		Plural All Genders
Nom.	welcher	who	welche	welches	which	welche
Acc.	welchen	whom	welche	welches	which	welche
Gen.	dessen	whose	deren	dessen	of which	deren
Dat.	welchem	to whom	welcher	welchem	to which	welchen

The resemblance of the above declension to the interrogative welcher is very plain. The genitive is the case that demands your attention.

The English meanings given above apply only to English nouns. If welches refers to a person it must be translated not *which*, but *who*.

> Das Mädchen, welches (or das) die Eier gekauft hat, ist jung.
> The maiden, *who* bought the eggs, is young.
> Die Stadt, die (or welche) er gerettet hatte, war sehr alt.
> The town, *which* he had saved, was very old.
> Er hat einen Teller gekauft, den (or welchen) er in der Stadt gesehen hatte. He has bought a plate, *which* he had seen in the city.

In all these examples you will observe the peculiar place of the verb in the clause to which the relative belongs. In all these clauses the personal verb is put *at the end*.

> Der Ritter, welchen Ihre Freunde gestern sahen, ist tot.
> The knight, whom your friends saw yesterday, is dead.

Observe the punctuation in the examples given: every relative sentence is enclosed between two commas.

In English we could, if we liked, leave out the *whom*, and say only, *the knight, your friends saw yesterday, is dead*. But in German this is NEVER allowed. The relative can never be omitted.

The genitive of the relative must always in German come *before* the noun to which it refers. We say in English, *the house the doors of which have fallen*. In German this must run, das Haus, dessen Türen gefallen sind. In other words, we must always use in German *whose* instead of *of which*. *Whose* always comes before its noun in English, and takes away the need of the article: thus, *a coat, of which the sleeve was torn*, should be put into German in the form, *a coat, whose sleeve was torn*. Here the article *the* is got rid of altogether.

When referring to things wo- or wor- followed by a

preposition may be used instead of the usual relative pronoun:

> Das Flugzeug, mit dem (or womit) er nach Deutschland flog, verunglückte. The aeroplane in which he was travelling to Germany crashed.

Was is used to translate *which* when referring to a whole clause, and also after the following: alles, everything; vieles, much; nichts, nothing:

> Es rieselte, was dem alten Fischer ausserordentlich gefiel. It was drizzling, which pleased the old fisherman immensely.
>
> Alles, was ich habe, everything I have.
>
> Nichts, was er sagte, nothing he said.

Vocabulary

der Arzt, doctor
der Metzger, butcher
der Chauffeur, chauffeur
die Stenotypistin, shorthand typist
der Zahn, tooth
der Zahnarzt, dentist
der Jäger, huntsman, hunter
der Dieb, thief, burglar
der Richter, judge
der Briefträger, postman
der Schuhflicker, cobbler
das Wirtshaus zum " Roten Löwen," Red Lion Inn
das Wirtshaus zur " Blauen Kuh," Blue Cow Inn
der Wirt, landlord, inn-keeper
der Film, film
die Rolle, roll, part
der Kunde, customer
das Kindermädchen, nurse-maid
der Korb, basket
die Schublade, drawer

der Schauspieler, actor
der Filmschauspieler, film actor
der Kaufmann, shopkeeper
der Schriftsteller, author
der Kellner, waiter
*bitten (um), to ask for
*werden, to become
Seemann werden, to become a sailor
Briefträger sein, to be a postman
*stehlen, to steal
heilen, to heal, to cure
*ziehen, pull, draw
verhaften, to arrest
reparieren, to mend
nach Diktat *schreiben, to take down
*treffen, to meet
bedienen, to serve
spazieren *gehen, to go for a walk
spazieren führen, to take for a walk

Exercise 40

Der Mann, mit dem ich gestern gesprochen habe, ist der Bürgermeister von Brüssel (Brussels). Eine grosse Filmschauspielerin spielt eine Rolle im Film, den wir heute abend sehen werden. Der Wirt des Wirtshauses zum " Roten Löwen " (der Wirt des " Roten Löwen "), in dem (wo, worin) ich gestern den Chauffeur des Film-schauspielers Willi Fritsch traf, ist Seemann (Matrose) gewesen. Der Schuhflicker, der deine braunen Schuhe repariert hat, ist an der Tür. Der Metzger bediente seine Kunden, unter (= amongst) denen die Magd eines grossen Schriftstellers war. Der Korb, in welchem (in dem, worin) sie die Äpfel und Nüsse trug, war ganz neu. Der Zahnarzt, in dessen Haus der Polizist den Dieb verhaftete, hat heute morgen meinen Zahn gezogen. Die Stenotypistin, die diesen Brief nach Diktat schrieb, ist tot.

Exercise 41

You will have seen from the foregoing how important the relative pronoun is, and how considerably it adds to our powers of self-expression. Descriptions which before were detached and awkward now come more naturally.

As an interesting departure from the usual type of exercise the student is asked to rewrite the following pairs of detached sentences, joining each pair by means of a relative pronoun.

We will do one as an example:

(i) Er fuhr das Auto. He was driving the car.
(ii) Das Auto schleuderte auf der nassen Strasse. The car skidded on the wet road.
(iii) Das Auto, das er fuhr, schleuderte auf der nassen Strasse. The car he was driving skidded on the wet road.

1. Der Briefträger hat einen Brief gebracht. Die Schwester des Briefträgers ist unser Kindermädchen. 2. Der Mann ist der Neffe eines grossen Richters. Ich

habe mit dem Manne gesprochen. 3. Die Schublade war fast leer. Ich sah den Brief in der Schublade. 4. Die Frau ist sehr reich. Wir sahen gestern ihren Mann in der " Blauen Kuh." 5. Der Kellner bediente den Jäger. Der Jäger ist bei einem sehr reichen Kaufmann angestellt. 6. Der Dieb ist der Bruder eines Polizisten. Der Dieb stahl die Armbanduhr einer grossen Filmschauspielerin. 7. Das Kino war gross und prachtvoll. Ich sah diesen Film in dem Kino. 8. Der Arzt ist nach Ägypten (Egypt) gegangen. Der Arzt hat meinen Neffen geheilt. 9. Die Brüder sind im Krankenhaus. Das Flugzeug der Brüder verunglückte.

Exercise 42

The two girls, whose father played a great part in the film " Michael Kohlhaas," were listening to the wireless. The letter which I saw in this drawer was from your brother. The nurse-maid who has taken the children for a walk is from Cologne. The doctor whose nephew I met yesterday cured my sister in Switzerland. The house in which he lived had a red roof and a green door. The shorthand typist who took this letter down has a brother who is employed at your uncle's. The man to whom I was speaking yesterday is the landlord of the " Jolly Farmer." The café in which we met him is near the post-office. Everything we saw was white. The postman has a letter which comes from Russia. At the station we saw (= saw we) the brothers who flew last year to America. The waiter whose brothers stole the actress's car was serving the policeman who arrested them. Nothing he does is very good. The weather was bright and warm, which made our work easy.

LESSON XV

ORDER OF WORDS

I. Verb before Subject

If a clause in German begins with an adverb, or an adverbial phrase, the verb and the subject in that clause change places. *Yesterday he was ill* becomes gestern war er krank.

Certain adverbial conjunctions have the power to cause the same change—*inversion* it is usually called—in the clauses they introduce. Some of the most common of these are:

also, so, therefore	jetzt *or* nun, now
auch, also, too	kaum, scarcely
dann, da, then	so, so (= thus)
doch, yet, however	vielmehr, rather

Now he was poor.	Nun war er arm.
Yet she killed her friend.	Doch tötete sie ihren Freund.

We are not to think this a remarkable thing in German. In English we cannot say: *Scarcely he was dead*; the order must be as in German: Kaum war er tot.

2. Verb at End of Clause

In German, however, this system of changed order is carried further. For all conjunctions which introduce dependent clauses have the peculiar effect of throwing the personal verb in the dependent clause to the very end of that clause.

Some of the commonest of such subordinating conjunctions are:

als, as, when (past time)	dass, that
wenn, when (pres. or fut.)	bis, until
wenn, whenever	sobald, as soon as
wenn, if	obgleich, although
ob, if, whether	weil, because

wie, as, how	indem, whilst
da, as, since	bevor, before
während, whilst	so dass, so that

Er weiss, dass die Kinder böse waren.   He knows that the children were wicked.

Die Mutter war krank, weil ihr Sohn sie sehr schlecht behandelte.   The mother was ill because her son treated her very badly.

Do not forget the comma!   This is most important.

Subordinate Clause + Main Clause

A subordinate clause may precede a main clause, whereas a co-ordinate one (*i.e.* with a conjunction which does not change the word order, like und, *and*, aber, *but*, denn, *for*, oder, *or*) cannot do so, and when this happens the first rule is applied, namely, when the subject does not begin the sentence the verb precedes the subject:

Als er nach Hause kam, sah er seinen Onkel.   When he came home he saw his uncle.

Vocabulary

der Fischer, fisherman	bauen, to build
der Fisch, fish	krank, ill
das Boot, boat [1]	die Erkältung, cold (illness)
der See (—s, —n), lake	*fangen, to catch
der Sekretär, secretary	*finden, to find
ins (or zu) Bett gehen, to go to bed	schneien, to snow
regnen, to rain	die Aufgabe, exercise
rudern, to row	*schliessen, to shut
müde, tired	

Exercise 43

Begin each of the following sentences with dann, then, bald, soon, gestern, yesterday, einmal, once, eines Tages, one day, or plötzlich, suddenly:

1. Ein armer Fischer wohnte in diesem Dorfe.   2. Wir trafen die Sekretärin des Schriftstellers am Bahnhof. 3. Die Russen bauten neue Schulen und Universitäten. 4. Der Hund lief aus dem Zimmer.   5. Der Schneider kam nach Hause.

[1] Pronunciation of Boot is, in phonetic symbols, bo:t (see p. 16).

Exercise 44

Join up each of the following pairs of sentences so as to make one good compound sentence, as this example shows:

(i) Meine Schwester spielte Klavier. My sister was playing the piano.
(ii) Ich schrieb einen Brief. I wrote a letter.
(iii) Meine Schwester spielte Klavier, während ich einen Brief schrieb. My sister played the piano while I wrote a letter.

You may find it convenient to use an adverbial conjunction instead of a subordinating one, or you may put your subordinate clause first.

1. Er ging ins Hospital. Er war krank. 2. Ich war nicht dort. Er kam nach Hause. 3. Ich werde den Brief schreiben. Ich komme nach Hause. 4. Ich werde meinen Freund besuchen. Ich gehe ins Kino. 5. Er trägt keinen Mantel. Es ist sehr kalt. 6. Wir hatten eine Erkältung. Wir gingen ins Bett. 7. Er war sehr reich. Er war sehr traurig. 8. Das Mädchen ging ins Bett. Sie war sehr müde. 9. Ich traf sie. Sie lächelte immer. 10. Ich öffnete die Schublade. Ich sah die Taschenuhr.

Exercise 45

It was raining when the fisherman rowed across (= over) the lake. He caught no fish (*plural*), as the fish were not hungry. My children were listening to the German children's songs on the wireless while I was writing this exercise. As soon as he comes home he will 'phone you. Did you not shut the doors before you went to bed? When I go [1] to Berlin I shall visit your uncle. As they were not at home we put the letter in the letter-box. It was snowing as we drove to the station. He speaks German, French, English and Italian,

[1] To go (in a vehicle), fahren (by, mit).

although he has never been in these countries. They worked until it was quite dark. When the maid came to the door the man asked for bread and tea. We went [1] by boat across the lake, although it was quite dark.

LESSON XVI

OTHER PRONOUNS

We must now learn the remaining personal pronouns:

1st Personal Pronoun

	Singular			Plural	
Nom.	ich	I		wir	we
Acc.	mich	me		uns	us
Dat.	mir	to me		uns	to us

2nd Personal Pronoun

	Singular			Plural		
Nom.	du	thou	Sie	you	⎧ihr⎫
Acc.	dich	thee	Sie	you	⎨euch⎬
Dat.	dir	to thee	Ihnen	to you	⎩euch⎭ [2]

He has told (to) me. Er hat mir gesagt.
He saw us. Er sah uns.
They saw you. Sie sahen Sie.
She gives (to) us a book. Sie gibt uns ein Buch.
Nobody saw me, but everybody saw you. Niemand sah mich, aber jedermann sah Sie.

Indefinite Pronouns

1. *Man* is a very useful word corresponding to the English *one, we, they, people, you*, used indefinitely and not referring to any particular person:

Man hat es mir gesagt. People have told me (*or* I have been told).

---

[1] See footnote, p. 83.
[2] These forms are the real plural of du, dich, dir.

Man can only be used in the nominative. In other cases the following pronoun is used.

2. Einer refers indefinitely to a single person or thing:

> Einer meiner Freunde, one of my friends.
> Ich gehe zu einem Restaurant, wo die Kellner einen schnell bedienen. I go to a restaurant where the waiters serve one quickly.

The English *one* is untranslated in German after an adjective:

> Ich habe keine Feder. Haben Sie eine? I haven't a pen. Have you one?
> But: Hier ist eine gute. Here is a good one.

3. Keiner, niemand. Both mean *none, no one, nobody*, and keiner also *none* in speaking of things:

> Ich habe kein Brot, und du hast auch keines. I have no bread and you have none also.
> Niemand (keiner) hat uns gesehen. Nobody saw us.

Note. Both einer and keiner are declined like welcher or dieser. Niemand takes -s or -es in the genitive, and may (but need not) take -en in the accusative and -em in the dative. In this respect it is just like jemand, which follows.

4. Jemand means *somebody, someone*.

5. Wer means *he who, whoever*, and sends the verb to the end:

> Wer das gesagt hat, lügt. He who (whoever) said that is lying.

6. Nichts, *nothing*, etwas, *something*.

7. Welcher, *some, any*.

> Ich habe keinen Zucker. Haben Sie welchen? I have no sugar. Have you any?
> Hast du kein warmes Wasser? Hier ist welches. Haven't you any warm water? Here is some.

Indefinite Adjectives *or* Pronouns

The following may be used either as adjectives *or* pronouns :

all, all (1)
ander-, ander, other (2)
beide, both
ein bisschen, a (very) little
ein paar, a few
einige, some, any (plur.)
etwas, some, any (sing.)
jeder, each, every, each one
genug, enough (3)

manch-, mancher, some, many,
   many a
mehr, more
mehrere, several
viel, much; (plur.), many (4)
wenig, little; (plur.), few (4)
keiner von beiden, neither
a few = einige or ein paar

1. Alles = *all, everything* (it may even replace alle (*pl.*) meaning *all, everybody*). *Which* or *that* after alles is rendered by was.

All the may be translated by ' all ' with the proper ending or by ' all ' + article. Before words like *his, my, this*, etc. ' all ' need not take an ending:

Alles, was er sagte.   Everything he said.
Er stahl all das Geld.   He stole all the money.
All meine Freunde.   All my friends.

All = the whole of = der ganze:

Die ganze Stadt.   All the town.

2. *Other = different*, ander-.
   Other = additional, noch (ein).

Dieses Buch ist nicht sehr gut.   Haben Sie ein anderes?
   This book is not very good.   Have you another one?
Hier sind nur zwei Bücher.   Haben Sie noch eines?   Here
   are only two books.   Have you another (one)?

3. Genug usually follows the noun:

Haben wir Zucker genug?   Have we enough sugar?

4. In the singular viel and wenig need not take an ending.   *A little* = ein wenig.

Vocabulary

die Mahlzeit, meal
das Frühstück, breakfast
das Mittagessen, lunch
das Abendessen, dinner
der Kaffee, coffee
das Brötchen, roll
die Butter, butter
der Käse,[1] cheese
die Milch, milk
die Suppe, soup
der Wein, wine
das Bier, beer
die Torte, cake
der Teller, plate
die Kanne, pot
der Speiseschrank, food-cupboard, larder
die Kartoffel, potato

die Karotte, carrot
die Bohne, bean
die Erbse, pea
das Eis, ice (cream)
das Bonbon (—s, —s), sweet
die Sahne, cream
die Kirsche, cherry
die Apfelsine, orange
die Banane, banana
die Zitrone, lemon
das Messer, knife
die Gabel, fork
der Löffel, spoon
die Tasse, cup
die Dose, bowl, basin, tin
pflücken, pluck, gather, pick
schläfrig, sleepy

Exercise 46

Der Dieb antwortete mir nicht. Hast du sie nicht am Bahnhof getroffen? Wer hat Ihnen dieses schöne Buch gegeben? Es sind viele Kirschen und Äpfel im Garten. Ja, ich habe sie schon gesehen. Ich werde meinem Freunde welche geben. Meine kleine Schwester bat mich um Bonbons. Ich gab ihr einige, aber sie hat sie schon gegessen. " Noch ein Glas, bitte! " sagte ich zum Kellner, aber er hörte mich nicht. Zu Weihnachten wird Onkel Fritz uns besuchen. Wir haben noch etwas Butter im Speiseschrank. Essen Sie gern Brötchen mit Butter und Käse? Wir haben keine Apfelsinen mehr. Trinken Sie Kaffee mit oder ohne Sahne? Mit Sahne, wenn Sie welche haben. Beide Brüder (die beiden Brüder) waren dort. Haben Sie keine anderen Bananen? Ich habe noch einige,[2] aber sie sind nicht reif. Ich werde dir ein Eis kaufen, wenn du mir einige Erbsen und Bohnen im Garten pflückst. Hast du noch etwas Tee in der Kanne? Ist jemand an der Tür? Ich sehe nie-

---

[1] 2nd Declension.
[2] noch einige (plur.), noch etwas (sing.), some more.

mand dort. Man hat alles gehört, was du mir gestern sagtest. Jeder (Ein jeder) im Dorfe hat seinen langen Garten, worin er Kartoffeln, Bohnen, Erbsen, Äpfel, Kirschen usw. hat. Man trinkt viel Kaffee in Deutschland. Ich hatte keinen Teller, aber der Kellner hat mir einen gebracht.

Exercise 47

People drink more tea in England. Have you any coffee in the larder? Yes, I have a little. If you haven't enough books I have another one here. Our uncle gave us some sweets and oranges. I like oranges. The huntsman drank another glass of [1] wine. There are some more potatoes in the garden, if you have not enough here. The Spanish girls were picking oranges and lemons, and they gave us some. Have you any milk or cream? The breakfast at the " Blue Cow " was fairly cheap, but the lunch at the " Red Lion " was very dear, and they gave us no coffee. I do not like cheese. Is there any more sugar in the basin? The waiter has brought me another knife, as this one is dirty. For (zum) dinner we shall have cherries and bananas with cream. The waiter will bring you some more soup. Everybody was sleepy but nobody went to bed. All his friends are in America. A few sheep were in the field. He speaks a (very) little German, but no Spanish. Who has eaten all the cherries?

LESSON XVII

AUXILIARIES OF MOOD—THE IMPERATIVE

There are six very important little verbs that now claim attention. They are generally used along with the Infinitives of other verbs, and so are called Auxiliaries.

[1] Of in such expressions is omitted.

Since they tell us something about the mode or manner in which an action is to be done, they are often called the Auxiliaries of *Mood*. You have already come across three of them in your reading.

	Infinitive	Imperfect	Past Part.	Pres. Ind.
to dare *or* to be permitted }	dürfen	durfte	gedurft	ich darf
to be able	können	konnte	gekonnt	ich kann
to be permitted to like }	mögen	mochte	gemocht	ich mag
to be obliged to	müssen	musste	gemusst	ich muss
to owe to, to be to	sollen	sollte	gesollt	ich soll
to be willing, to wish	wollen	wollte	gewollt	ich will

There is little difficulty in dealing with these verbs, as they are good-natured enough to be very regular. The Present Indicative of each is given below. You will observe that the plural is always the same as the Infinitive:

1.	ich	darf, I may	kann, I can	mag, I may[1]
2.	du	darfst	kannst	magst
3.	er	darf	kann	mag
1.	wir	dürfen	können	mögen
2. {	Sie	dürfen	können	mögen
	ihr	dürft	könnt	mögt
3.	sie	dürfen	können	mögen
1.	ich	muss, I must	soll, I am to	will, I will
2.	du	musst	sollst	willst
3.	er	muss	soll	will
1.	wir	müssen	sollen	wollen
2. {	Sie	müssen	sollen	wollen
	ihr	müsst	sollt	wollt or wollet
3.	sie	müssen	sollen	wollen

For the other tenses these verbs are treated exactly like ordinary verbs. Thus the Perfect of müssen is ich habe gemusst = I have musted, *i.e.* I have been obliged to. But when these verbs are used with the Infinitive of another verb they take the form of the Infinitive

---

[1] The student is advised to *avoid* the use of mögen at this stage. Mögen also means *to like*.

instead of the Past Participle in the Perfect tenses. Thus " I have been obliged to wait " runs ich habe warten müssen.

The Imperative

When we order or command we are said to use the Imperative mood. Tanzen is *to dance*, tanze is the order *dance!* if given to one person, tanzet if to more than one person. These two forms are used only in addressing near relations, intimate friends and children.

The ordinary form of the Imperative, both in speaking to one person and to several persons, is tanzen Sie!

Singular (familiar)		Plural (familiar)	Singular and Plural (ordinary or polite form)
suche	seek	suchet	suchen Sie
lege	lay *or* place	leget	legen Sie
arbeite	work	arbeitet	arbeiten Sie
antworte	answer	antwortet	antworten Sie

Geben Sie mir ein Buch ! Give me a book.
Senden Sie ihr den Vogel ! Send her the bird.

Let us go. { Gehen wir !
Lass [1] uns gehen !
Wir wollen gehen.

See also p. 135.

Vocabulary

der Zug, train
der Autobus, 'bus
die Elektrische } tram
die Strassenbahn
die Tankstelle, petrol station
das Benzin, petrol
der Benzinbehälter, petrol-tank
das Motorrad, motor-cycle

das Rad, wheel, (bike)
die Hupe, horn
die Bremse, brake
die Einbahnstrasse, one-way street
eine Radfahrt machen, to go for a cycle-ride [2]
eine Autofahrt, motor-ride

---

[1] It all depends on whom we are addressing :
Lass uns gehen ! (du).
Lassen Sie uns gehen ! (Sie).
Lasst uns gehen ! (ihr).
[2] Similarly with Autofahrt, Bootfahrt.

eine Bootfahrt, a boat trip
die Taxe \
die Autodroschke } taxi
gleich, immediately
rückwärts, backwards
gut, good or well
besteigen, to board
winken, to beckon, signal
*verlassen, to leave
*rufen, to call, shout
das Fahrrad, bicycle
auf dem Fahrrad fahren, to cycle
Rad fahren, to cycle
das Flugzeug, aeroplane
der Reifen, tyre
der Verkehrsschutzmann,
    traffic policeman
zu Fuss gehen,[1] to go on foot

mit dem Zug fahren,[2] to go by
    train
versäumen, to miss
platzen, to burst
*steigen, to mount, climb
*halten, to stop
in Ordnung, in proper order
parken, to park (vehicle)
das Parken ist verboten, park-
    ing is forbidden
überholen, to overtake
*scheinen, to shine, to seem
langsam, slow, slowly
eilen, to hurry
sonst, otherwise
fragen, to ask
der Weg, way
böse, bad

Exercise 48

Der Vater sagte zu den Kindern: " Wollt ihr heute
abend eine Autofahrt nach Berlin machen? " " O ja,
gerne! " riefen die Kinder. Sie mussten ihre neuen
Anzüge tragen, weil sie ihre Kusinen und Vettern in
Berlin besuchen sollten. Sie konnten das Haus nicht vor
drei Uhr verlassen, weil die Mutter nicht fertig war.
" Kann ich nach Berlin auf dem Rad fahren? " fragte der
junge Karl. " O nein! " antwortete der Vater. " Auf
dem Rad geht es viel zu langsam. Du musst mit uns
kommen."

Bald waren sie alle fertig. Der Vater kann sehr gut
führen. " Ich muss mehr Benzin kaufen," sagte er, " der
Benzinbehälter ist fast leer." Also hielten sie an einer
Tankstelle. Dann kamen sie zu einer Strassenkreuzung.
Dort war rotes Licht und sie mussten warten. Herrn
Schmidts Auto kann sehr gut steigen und sie fuhren sehr
schnell auf dem Wege nach Berlin. Um halb vier waren

---

[1] Gehen strictly speaking is *to walk*, and when a vehicle is
mentioned or implied, fahren should be used.

[2] To travel *by* a vehicle is in German to drive *with*.

sie in Berlin. Dort sahen Sie einen armen Motorradfahrer, der einen geplatzten Reifen reparierte. Auf den breiten Strassen Berlins sahen sie Autobusse, Elektrische, Autos, Taxen und Fahrräder. Dort ist der Verkehr sehr gefährlich. Sie fuhren in eine Einbahnstrasse, also haben sie rückwärts fahren müssen. Über der Stadt sahen sie ein grosses Flugzeug, das nach Amerika fliegen sollte. Viele Fussgänger eilten über die Strasse, und es war gut, dass die Hupe in Ordnung war. Aber sie konnten immer ziemlich schnell fahren und überholten viele andere Autos. Dann hielt das Auto, und Herr Schmidt winkte einem Verkehrsschutzmann. Er hat nach [1] dem Wege fragen müssen. Bald aber waren sie vor dem Hause des Onkels.

Exercise 49

You can go to Berlin if you want to. I am to visit the dentist this evening. May [2] I smoke here? I will [3] take my dog for a walk in the park. He was to fly to Paris yesterday (= yesterday to Paris), but suddenly became ill. We had to walk home. As he could not speak German he took me with him. You are to go immediately to bed. German is spoken here (= here one speaks German). Shall [4] I buy some bread? You are to talk to (= to speak with) nobody. We could not see the aeroplane on account of the fog. May we go to the cinema this evening? We had to go by taxi. If the weather is warm you may bathe in the lake this afternoon (= this afternoon in the lake—always *Time* before *Place*). We want to see your cows and sheep. I cannot tell you (it). As my brother is unable to visit you, he is sending you a letter.

[1] To ask for = to demand, bitten um; = to inquire about, fragen nach.

[2] *May* in questions and negative statements : use dürfen.

[3] When *will* means *want to* rather than just a future action, use wollen.

[4] When *shall* has the meaning of *am I to*, use sollen.

Exercise 50

Take (= carry) this letter to the post. Let us go for a walk round the town. I have had [1] to go to Berlin. She has had to learn Spanish. They have not been able to find your book. He is to leave London to-morrow (Time before Place!). Have you (du) been able to see this film? He would not (= did not want to) answer. My sisters had to go by air (= travel with the aeroplane). I cannot speak Swedish. Can she speak Dutch? We have not been able to send you many apples, as the summer has been too bad. We could not travel very quickly, on account of the fog. You can go by bus to the station. Will you sing us a song? I cannot sing, as I have a bad cold.

Exercise 51

Kellner,[2] bringen Sie uns zwei Glas [3] Bier, bitte! Chauffeur, fahren Sie schnell zum Bahnhof! Geben Sie mir bitte ein Eis. Gehen wir ins Kino! Bitte, wiegen Sie diesen Brief für mich! Reichen Sie mir bitte den Zucker! Lasst uns heute abend ins Theater gehen! Öffnen Sie bitte die Tür! Frage den Schutzmann (den Polizisten) nach dem Wege! Wir wollen morgen nach London gehen! Bitte, sagen Sie mir, wo ich eine Taxe finden kann. Kaufen Sie mir einige Zigaretten! Geben Sie mir eine Londoner Zeitung!

---

[1] *I have had to* may be rendered either by ich habe . . . sollen or ich habe . . . müssen. Sollen implies *duty* or *obligation*, müssen indicates *necessity*.

[2] Recently it has become customary to address a waiter as Ober ! or Herr Ober ! (Oberkellner, strictly speaking, is the *head waiter*, but in calling a waiter this form of flattery is adopted.)

[3] Notice that in such expressions, where the English *of* is omitted, a *masculine* or *neuter* noun does not take the plural form. A *feminine* noun does, *e.g.*

zwei Flaschen Wein, two bottles of wine (die Flasche, *bottle*).

LESSON XVIII

SEPARABLE AND INSEPARABLE VERBS

1. The Separable Prefix

In English we have the word *upset*. This is composed of two separate words, *up* and *set*. But we cannot separate these words without changing the meaning of the whole. *Set up* means something very different from *upset*.

Now in German we have two kinds of verbs made up of a verb and another word. To the first class belong what are called separable verbs, because the two parts can be separated; the others are called inseparable, because the two parts must always be kept together.

The peculiarities of separable verbs are these:

1. In the Present and Imperfect Indicative and in the Imperative the separable little word is taken away from the front of the verb and put at the end of the sentence. Thus, zurückkommen means *to come back*; so we have the sentence, da kamen wir nach London zurück. In the same way, kommen Sie zurück means *come back*.

2. In the Past Participle and in the Infinitive the ge- and zu- are put between the two parts of separable verbs, losgelassen and zurückzukommen. Er wünschte zurückzukommen = he wished to come back.

3. In pronouncing the word more stress is laid upon the separable part, thus: zurück'kommen, los'lassen.

Here are some separable verbs to practise on:

*ankommen, to arrive	*einsteigen, to get in (vehicle)
*aufstehen, to get up	*wegnehmen, to take away
*ausgehen, to go out	abreisen, to set out
*fortfahren, to go on	zumachen, to shut

It is to be noted that separable verbs do not separate their prefix unless in *independent* sentences. I come back soon = ich komme bald zurück. But for "if I come back soon" we write, wenn ich bald zurückkomme.

2. The Inseparable Prefix

The very fact that certain verbs are called *separable* leads us to expect that certain other verbs are called *inseparable*. Those inseparable verbs are made up of two parts just like the separable, but the prefixes are never separated from the rest of the verb. The prefixes that cannot be separated from the rest of the verb are: be-, emp-, ent-, er-, ge-, hinter-, miss-, ver-, voll-, wider-, zer-.

*behalten, to keep
*empfangen, to receive
*entscheiden, to decide
*erschrecken, to be frightened (vor, at)
gebrauchen, to use, to employ

*hinterlassen, to leave
*missfallen, to displease
*vergessen, to forget
*vollbringen, to accomplish
*widerstehen, to resist
*zerbrechen, to break

Besides the quality which gives them their name—that of retaining the prefixes joined to the verb in all cases—these inseparable verbs have the following three characteristics:

1. They do not admit of the prefix ge- in the Past Participle. We say ich habe vergessen (not gevergessen).

2. The zu of the Infinitive is put before the prefix: as zu misshandeln.

3. The accent is placed not on the prefix but on the root part of the verb.

3. Some Special Cases

There are four prefixes—durch-, über-, unter- and um- —that give a good deal of trouble, because they are sometimes separable and sometimes inseparable.

The test is: Does the preposition have its usual meaning along with the verb? If it has, the compound is a separable verb; if it has not, the compound is an inseparable verb. Umgehen may mean " to go about,"

" to lounge about," " to go round." In these cases um-
has clearly retained its ordinary meaning, so it is separable. I go about with my neighbour = ich gehe mit
meinem Nachbar um, *i.e.* I associate with him. But
umgehen also means to elude, to avoid. Here um- has
not its literal meaning: it is used figuratively, so the
verb is inseparable. I avoid it = ich umgehe es.

In actual speech the separable forms accent the durch-,
über-, unter- and um-, the inseparables accent the root
of the verb. Thus: ü'bersetzen = to set over; über-
se'tzen = to translate.

The inseparables form one class of verbs that do not
have ge- in the Past Participle. There is another, and
rather an important class. If any new verb comes into
English we at once make it into a regular verb by adding
-ed for both Past and Past Participle: *Telegraph, telegraphed, telegraphed.* The Germans just as naturally
make the verb end in -ieren and we have telegraphieren,
telegraphierte, telegraphiert; so with *telephone*: tele-
phonieren, telephonierte, telephoniert. Most new German
verbs, especially those derived from the classical languages
and from the French, end in -ieren; and all German verbs
ending in -ieren have no ge- in the Past Participle, and
have the ordinary -te in the Past: studieren, studierte,
studiert = to study; marschieren, marschierte, mar-
schiert = to march. The reason for the omission of the
ge- is that in these verbs, and in inseparable verbs, the
first syllable is not accented.

Notice carefully the order of the separable prefix:

Ich gehe	jeden Tag	aus.	I go out every day.
Ich ging	,,	aus.	I went out every day.
Ich bin	,,	ausgegangen.	I have been out every day.
Ich werde	,,	ausgehen.	I shall go out every day.
Ich will	,,	ausgehen.	I want to go out every day.
Ich wünsche	,,	auszugehen.	I desire to go out every day.
Da ich	,,	ausging.	As I went out every day.

The Particles Hin and Her

These particles are frequently added to form a compound with the verb or with a separable prefix in order further to define the *direction*.

Hin expresses a *direction away* from the point of view, her a *movement towards* it.   Everything depends on the point from which we " project " the description.   For instance, if we describe a man walking along the street and say he entered a house, we may take the point of view of the man in the street and say hin, or the point of view inside the house and say her.

These particles are very important and should be constantly studied and practised.

Note the following:

> (Kommen Sie) herein ! Come in ! (Einkommen is to *come in, enter*.)
> Gehen Sie hinaus !   Go out ! (Ausgehen, *to go out*.)
> Wir gingen die Strasse hinauf.   We went up the street.
> Er kam die Strasse herunter.   He came down the street.

It follows that a person going anywhere will himself say hin, as he must be going to a place away from him, and a verb like kommen usually takes her.

The English *there* and *where*

These particles are often used to complete the sense of direction, a fine point that is often lacking in English. The words *there* and *where* are therefore dort (da) or dorthin (dahin), wo or wohin, according as the meaning is *there* (in that place) or *thither* (to that place), or *where* (in what place) or *whither* (to what place):

> Wohin gehen Sie (Wo gehen Sie hin)?   Where are you going?
> Wo ist das Buch?   Where is the book?
> Er ging dorthin.   He went there.
> Er steht dort.   He is standing there.
> Er legte das Buch hin.   He put the book down.
> Der Junge fiel hin.   The boy fell (down).

D

Vocabulary

das Gepäck, luggage
der Träger, porter
der Gepäckraum, cloak-room
der Erfrischungsraum, refreshment-room
der Schaffner, guard
die Lokomotive, engine
der Wagen, carriage
das Abteil, compartment
das Raucherabteil, smoking compartment
das Nichtraucherabteil, non-smoking compartment
der Schalter, ticket-office
die Rolltreppe, escalator
die Karte, ticket
die Bahnsteigkarte, platform ticket
die Hinfahrtskarte, single (ticket)
die Rückfahrkarte, return (ticket)
die Verbindung, connection
der Speisewagen, dining-car
*lassen, to leave (thing)
*verlassen, to leave (person or place)
frei, free, vacant
besetzt, occupied, taken
abholen, to meet (from the station)
*fahren, to run (of trains)
*pfeifen, to whistle
rechtzeitig, punctual (ly)
Einsteigen! Take your seats, please!
*zurückgehen, to go back, return
*lesen, to read

sonst, otherwise
der Automat, ticket-machine
der Gepäckwagen, luggage-van
der Platz, place, seat
der Abort, lavatory
der Gang, corridor
das Netz, rack
der Ausgang, exit
der Wartesaal, waiting-room
der Bücherstand, bookstall
der Bahnsteig, platform
das Trinkgeld, " tip "
der Koffer, suit-case
das Köfferchen, attaché-case
der D-Zug, through train
der Zuschlag, extra (charge)
der Schlafwagen, sleeping-car
der Aufenthalt, stop
der Fahrplan, timetable
der Schnellzug, fast train
der Eckplatz, corner-seat
*eintreten, to enter
*einsteigen, to enter (vehicle)
hinauslehnen, to lean out
*ankommen, to arrive
*abfahren, to leave, depart
*aussteigen, to alight
*umsteigen, to change
holen, to fetch
versäumen, to miss
verspätet, delayed, late
zeigen, to show
furchtbar, terribly
Alles umsteigen ! All change !
*zurückkommen, to come back, return
gähnen, to yawn
hinsetzen, to put down

Exercise 52

Müllers [1] wollten nach Köln fahren. Sie suchten einen Schnellzug im Fahrplan. Ihr Gepäck war ganz fertig.

[1] The Müllers.

Sie fuhren mit der Taxe zum Bahnhof. Herr Müller
kaufte die Karten am Schalter. Sie mussten zum Bahnsteig neun eilen. Der Gepäckträger trug das Gepäck.
Hilde kaufte einige Bonbons und Frau Müller wählte
vom Bücherstand einige Zeitungen. Da der Zug verspätet war, warteten sie ein bisschen im Wartesaal.
Dann fuhr der Zug herein. Der Träger setzte das
Gepäck in den Gepäckwagen und Herr Müller gab ihm
ein Trinkgeld. Sie stiegen alle in ein leeres Abteil
hinein. Hilde und Max wählten die Eckplätze, da sie
zum Fenster hinaussehen wollten. Herr Müller legte
sein Köfferchen auf das Netz.

Die Lokomotive pfiff und dann fuhren sie ab. Da sie
in einem Raucherabteil waren, begann Herr Müller zu
rauchen. Er raucht gern Zigaretten. In Aachen [1]
mussten sie umsteigen. Um halb eins gingen sie den
Gang entlang [2] zum Speisewagen. Nach dem Mittagessen gingen sie zu ihrem Abteil zurück. Max musste
zum Abort gehen, weil seine Hände furchtbar schmutzig
waren. Herr Müller gähnte. Er war müde und begann
zu schlafen. Als sie rechtzeitig in Köln ankamen,
stiegen sie schnell aus. Auf dem Bahnhof sahen sie
Onkel Otto und Tante Gisela. Ein Träger holte ihr
Gepäck vom Gepäckwagen. Herr Müller gab die Karten
ab und sie verliessen den Bahnhof. Sie fuhren eine
lange, enge Strasse hinauf und kamen am Hause des
Onkels an. Sie traten ins Haus hinein. Sie waren alle
müde und hungrig.

Exercise 53

Give me three singles for (nach) Stettin, please! Do
not lean out of the window! Porter, take my luggage
to the fast train for Cologne, please. Driver (Taxi),
drive quickly to the station, otherwise I shall miss the

---

[1] Aix-la-Chapelle.
[2] Entlang, *along*, follows the noun in the accusative.

train for Coblence (Koblenz). Must I change in Aix-la-Chapelle? I left the house at half-past six.[1] All the seats were occupied. We returned last Monday to Berlin. Is there (omit *there*) a seat vacant for me? The through-train leaves at 9.30.[2] Aunt Marie met her at (von) the station. Did you miss the connection at Kassel? A tall man entered the room and spoke to me. My hat is in the dining-car. If you travel by this fast train you will have to pay extra. Put your case down. Where are you going? Where have you put your gloves? Where are the tickets?

LESSON XIX

CARDINAL NUMBERS

We have already had the numbers from one up to twenty. Now we must have the others. Old-fashioned people among ourselves still say *five-and-twenty* for 25. This is the regular way in German.

21	einundzwanzig	50	fünfzig
22	zweiundzwanzig	53	dreiundfünfzig
23	dreiundzwanzig	60	sechzig (note the s omitted)
24	vierundzwanzig	64	vierundsechzig
25	fünfundzwanzig	70	siebzig
26	sechsundzwanzig	75	fünfundsiebzig
27	siebenundzwanzig	80	achtzig
28	achtundzwanzig	86	sechsundachtzig
29	neunundzwanzig	90	neunzig
30	dreissig	97	siebenundneunzig
31	einunddreissig	100	hundert
40	vierzig	101	hundert und eins
42	zweiundvierzig	102	hundert und zwei

The hundreds go quite regularly, zweihundert, dreihundert, vierhundert, and so on. So with the thousands: Tausend = 1 000, zweitausend = 2 000, dreitausend = 3 000, etc. In a general way *a* hundred and *a* thousand

[1] um halb sieben.   [2] um halb zehn.

are simply hundert and tausend *without* the ein. But if we want to speak of one hundred or one thousand we say einhundert and eintausend (one word in each case) respectively. A million is eine Million (with accent on the on).

Here follow some examples of big numbers expressed in words:

123 = hundert dreiundzwanzig.
947 = neunhundert siebenundvierzig.
304 = dreihundert und vier.
1 032 = (ein) tausend zweiunddreissig.
1 870 = (ein) tausend achthundert siebzig or achtzehnhundert (und) siebzig.
1 900 = (ein) tausend neunhundert or neunzehnhundert.
1 563 825 = eine Million fünfhundertdreiundsechzigtausend achthundert fünfundzwanzig.

Hundert and tausend when used alone (*i.e.* not as adjectives) are regarded as nouns, and form their plural nominative and accusative by adding -e and dative by adding -en.

The simple arithmetical processes are as follows:

zweimal drei ist sechs	$= 2 \times 3 = 6$
drei und vier ist sieben	$= 3 + 4 = 7$
neun geteilt durch drei ist drei	$= 9 \div 3 = 3$
dreissig weniger zwanzig ist zehn	$= 30 - 20 = 10$

ORDINAL NUMBERS

The numbers we have been dealing with up till now are called *cardinal* numbers, because all other numbers *hinge* upon them—*cardo, cardinis,* being Latin for a *hinge.* But we sometimes want to express the *order* in which things occur, and then we use what are called the *ordinal* numbers—first, second, third, fourth, fifth, sixth, etc. You note that the first three end differently from all the rest. Just as we make a cardinal number into an ordinal by adding -*th*, so the Germans do the same thing by adding -te. Thus vierte, fünfte, sechste, and so on up to neunzehnte. 1st and 3rd are irregular, erste and dritte; 2nd is quite regular, zweite.

From 20 onwards all the numbers add -ste: 20th = zwanzigste; 90th = neunzigste; 100th = hundertste; 1,000th = tausendste.

But if a large number ends with a German number between one and nineteen inclusive it ends in -te: 112th = hundertundzwölfte; 1,010th = tausendundzehnte.

The -te or the -ste are the ordinary endings of adjectives, and only the parts of numbers which have these terminations are declined.

> He has chosen the 101st man.   Er hat den hundertundersten
>   Mann gewählt.
> His fifth attempt, sein fünfter Versuch.

There are certain very useful terminations used in connection with numbers:

1. -erlei when added means of so many kinds: zweierlei dreierlei, achterlei, hunderterlei = of two kinds, of three kinds, of eight kinds, of a hundred kinds respectively; allerlei = of all kinds; vielerlei = of many kinds.

2. -mal means so many times: einmal = once; fünfmal = five times; zehnmal = ten times; tausendmal = a thousand times.

3. -fach means so many fold: einfach = onefold (it also means *simple*); vierfach = fourfold; hundertfach = a hundredfold.

4. -ns when added to the ordinal numbers gives meanings corresponding to our " -ly " in numbers: erstens = firstly; zweitens = secondly; sechstens = sixthly, and so on.

5. -tel when added to the ordinals gives the forms corresponding to our fractions: das Drittel = the third; das Viertel = the fourth; das Sechstel = the sixth. For anything above 19 the ending is -stel: das Dreissigstel. $\frac{3}{4}$ = drei Viertel; $\frac{5}{7}$ = fünf Siebentel; $\frac{13}{20}$ = dreizehn Zwanzigstel.

DATES AND LETTERS

In order to deal with dates we must learn the names of the days of the week and the months of the year.

Das Jahr = the year; der Monat = the month; die Woche = the week.

January	Januar	May	Mai	September	Septem'ber
February	Februar	June	Juni	October	Okto'ber
March	März	July	Juli	November	Novem'ber
April	April'	August	August'	December	Dezem'ber

Sunday	Sonntag	Tuesday	Dienstag	Thursday	Donnerstag
Monday	Montag	Wednesday	Mittwoch	Friday	Freitag

Saturday Samstag or Sonnabend

Our English way of saying *of a Sunday* or *on Sundays* is represented in German by merely adding an -s to the day of the week we refer to.

On before a day of the week is translated an dem, contracted into am: am Samstag = on Saturday; am Sonntag = on Sunday.

The words for the months and days are all masculine in German, as are also the words for the four seasons.

Spring, der Frühling   Autumn, der Herbst
Summer, der Sommer   Winter, der Winter

In before a month or a season is translated by in dem, contracted into im: im Juli = in July; im Frühling = in spring.

But if we express a particular day of the month we use am. Thus:

On the 5th of November, am fünften November.
On the 18th of June in the year 1815, am achtzehnten Juni im Jahre achtzehnhundert fünfzehn.

Dates are also expressed by the accusative of the article without a preposition, as: den vierten Juli = on the 4th of July.

The hours of the day are represented by a numeral and the feminine word Uhr always in the singular: 11 o'clock

= elf Uhr; 4 o'clock = vier Uhr. We know that auf
means *direction towards* and nach means *after*, so we are
not surprised to find that ein Viertel auf sechs and ein
Viertel nach fünf mean the same thing: *a quarter past
five*. Similarly, drei Viertel auf drei and ein Viertel vor
drei both can stand for a quarter to three. Scottish
students will recognise an old friend in the phrase halb
vier = half-four: this means half *towards* four, and therefore means half-past three. The most usual way with
minutes is to use the number with nach up to the half-
hour *past*, and the number with vor from the half-hour
up to the next hour. Thus: 4.25 p.m. will be nachmittags um fünfundzwanzig Minuten nach vier; 4.35
a.m. will be morgens um fünfundzwanzig Minuten vor
fünf. When anything is done *at* a certain time we use
the preposition um, as um zehn Uhr = at 10 o'clock.
The question, *What o'clock is it?* is put Wieviel Uhr ist es?

The student should endeavour to get into touch
with a German living in Germany who would be willing
to correspond with him. This gives an added interest
to his studies and by correcting each other's mistakes
the correspondence can be beneficial to both sides.

How to begin a letter:

(Die Adresse)
den 15. Juli 1938.

(Die Anschrift):

Lieber Karl! — Dear Charles,
Mein lieber Heinrich! — My dear Henry,
Liebe Käthi! — Dear Kathleen,
Meine liebste Ottilie! — My dearest Ottilie,

Not so intimate:

Lieber Herr Klein! — Dear Mr. Small,
Liebe Frau Schmidt! — Dear Mrs. Smith,
Sehr geehrtes Fräulein Braun! — Dear Miss Brown,
Geehrter Herr Doktor! — Dear Doctor ——.

Besten (Schönen) Dank für Ihren Brief (Ihre Karte) vom 3.
März. Many thanks for your letter (card) of the 3rd March.

Ihren interessanten Brief vom 9. April habe ich gestern
   erhalten. Besten Dank! I received your interesting
   letter of the 9th April yesterday. Many thanks.
Ich lege Ihnen hiermit ein neues Bild von mir (von meinem
   Haus, von meinem Hund) bei. I enclose a new photo of
   myself (of my house, my dog).

How to end a letter:

Mit schönem Gruss an Sie und Ihre werte Frau, with best
   wishes to you and your wife.
Meine Schwester lässt Sie herzlich grüssen, my sister sends
   you her kind regards.
Mit den freundlichsten Grüssen, with sincerest wishes.
In der Hoffnung, bald im Besitz Ihrer Antwort zu sein.
   Hoping to get your answer shortly.

Ihr (Stets Ihr),	Yours truly (sincerely),
N.	N.

More formal and business-like:

Hochachtungsvoll,	Yours faithfully,
J. B.	J. B.

b.w. ! = bitte wenden ! = P.T.O.
N.S. (or P.S.) = P.S.

How to address the envelope:

> Herrn O. Hasenwinkel,
> Recklinghausen,
> Kellerstrasse 13.

> Fräulein Ottilie Weissdorn,
> bei Herrn Dr. Leineweber,
> Rostock,
> Wilhelmstr. 10.

Bitte nachsenden ! Please forward.
Eilt sehr ! Urgent !
Wenn unbestellbar, zurück an N. In case of non-delivery,
   please return to N.

Exercise 54

Write in full or read quickly:

(a)

$2 \times 3 = ?$	$5 + 3 = ?$
$4 \times 5 = ?$	$9 + 6 = ?$
$5 \times 6 = ?$	$19 + 17 = ?$
$7 \times 3 = ?$	$13 + 14 = ?$
$11 \times 11 = ?$	$43 + 38 = ?$

$27 \div 3 = ?$	$98 - 57 = ?$
$81 \div 9 = ?$	$139 - 87 = ?$
$44 \div 4 = ?$	$1\,716 - 741 = ?$
$121 \div 11 = ?$	$3\,921 - 1\,964 = ?$
$250 \div 50 = ?$	$1\,888 - 777 = ?$

(b) Um

9.0	6.30	12.0	1.40
2.45	3.20	12.10	10.45
11.10	3.50	1.0	5.30
5.45	7.15	1.20	8.15

(c) $\frac{1}{3}$, $\frac{2}{5}$, $\frac{4}{9}$, $\frac{1}{2}$, $\frac{3}{4}$, $\frac{5}{8}$, $\frac{6}{25}$;

1st, 2nd, 6th, 8th, 7th, 11th, 12th, 18th, 24th, 17th, 30th, 29th, 100th, 1000th.

LESSON XX

COMPARISON

When we compare two things in English we are said to use the *Comparative* degree of the adjective. I am stronger than you: here *stronger* is the Comparative, and is clearly formed by merely adding *-er* to the ordinary form of the adjective. In German we do exactly the same. Stark means *strong*, and we have already used stärker for *stronger*. Ich bin stärker als Sie = I am stronger than you. In addition to adding -er, however, the Germans (in the case of monosyllables) generally modify the vowel if it happens to be a, o, or u.

When more than two things are compared, we use what is called the *Superlative* degree of the adjective. This is indicated in English by the ending -*est*, as in *strongest*; the German ending is practically the same as in English; it is -st. Thus: *strongest* should be stärkst, but since the Superlative is always used with the article or some demonstrative word it never in practice ends baldly in -st, but must have the usual termination of an adjective used attributively.

> Der stärkste Mann, the strongest man.
> Mein stärkster Freund, my strongest friend.
> Dieser Mann ist am stärksten, this man is strongest.

When an adjective ends in d, t, s, ss, sch or z, or a vowel, there is an e put in before the st, making it exactly like English: hart = hard; härtest = hardest; treu, faithful, treuest, most faithful.

The ordinary form of the adjective is called the Positive; so we have the following table drawn up under three heads:

	Positive	Comparative	Superlative		
poor	arm	ärmer	(der or die or das)		ärmste
old	alt	älter	,,	,,	älteste
broad	breit	breiter	,,	,,	breiteste
stupid	dumm	dümmer	,,	,,	dümmste
noble	edel	edler	,,	,,	edelste
early	früh	früher	,,	,,	früheste
bad	schlecht	schlechter	,,	,,	schlechteste
brave	tapfer	tapf(e)rer	,,	,,	tapferste

You will note that adjectives ending in -el, -en, -er leave out the e in the Comparative. The -er and the -en adjectives *may* keep the e, but the -el ones usually drop it. The best plan is to drop it always in all three cases, and thus save confusion.

The following one-syllabled adjectives do *not* take the Umlaut in comparison:

false	falsch	falscher	falschest
happy	froh	froher	frohest
clear	klar	klarer	klarst
slim	schlank	schlanker	schlankst
flat	flach	flacher	flachst
bald	kahl	kahler	kahlst
round	rund	runder	rundest
proud	stolz	stolzer	stolzest
full	voll	voller	vollst
true	wahr	wahrer	wahrst
tender	zart	zarter	zartest

In German, as in all languages, some of the commonest adjectives are quite irregular. The following list should be learnt thoroughly:

	Positive	Comparative	Superlative
good	gut	besser	(der or die or das) beste
great	gross	grösser	„ „ grösste
high	hoch [1]	höher	„ „ höchste
near	nahe	näher	„ „ nächste

We have seen already that adjectives are frequently used as adverbs; and now we have to call attention to a peculiar adverbial form of the Superlative that may be called the Absolute Superlative, and is used predicatively with the verb sein. It has always the same form, and its termination does not change: am besten = the best; am grössten = the greatest; am edelsten = the noblest. You will understand its use from the following examples:

She is the most beautiful lady in the town. Sie ist die schönste Dame in der Stadt.

This lady is most beautiful in the morning. Diese Dame ist morgens am schönsten.

The just way is the best. Der gerade Weg ist der beste.

This way is best in spring. Dieser Weg ist im Frühling am besten.

---

[1] When an e follows, the c is always omitted :
Ein hoher Baum, a tall tree.
Ein höherer Baum, a taller tree.

It is plain that the am besten form is used when there is really no comparison with other things in the same sentence. It states that the quality of the adjective exists in the highest degree in the subject of the sentence. In this form there is no noun implied as following the adjective, whereas in the der beste form there is an implied noun: der gerade Weg ist der beste (Weg).

There are three kinds of comparison, each of which deserves attention:

1. Comparison indicating *equality*: this is expressed by (eben) so . . . wie.

> I am as good as you. Ich bin so gut wie Sie.
> The boy was as brave as his father. Der Knabe war ebenso tapfer wie sein Vater.

2. Comparison involving *inferiority* in respect of the quality indicated by the adjective. In this case we use the form nicht so . . . wie; *i.e.* the eben is omitted.

> You are not so bad as she. Sie sind nicht so schlecht wie sie.
> He is not as clever as his sister. Er ist nicht so geschickt wie seine Schwester.

3. Comparison involving *superiority* in respect of the quality indicated by the adjective. This is the commonest form, and is expressed by the ordinary comparative followed by als.

> The son was stronger than his father. Der Sohn war stärker als sein Vater.

4. When two adjectives refer to the same subject, the form with mehr is usual:

> He is more sly than clever. Er ist mehr schlau als klug.

The peculiar expression, *the* so-and-so *the* so-and-so, is expressed in German by je . . . desto or je . . . je.

> The older a man is the wiser he is. Je älter ein Mann ist, desto klüger ist er.

Note the construction; je requires the verb to be thrown to the end, desto requires inversion of verb.

The more the better, je mehr desto besser.
The longer the better, je länger je lieber.

When there is only one *the* with the comparative it is rendered by desto or um so.

The better for you, desto besser für Sie, *or* um so besser für Sie.

The Adverb

Many adverbs (saying how a thing is done) have the same form as the corresponding adjectives, *e.g.*:

Das Mädchen ist schön.   The girl is *beautiful*.
Das Mädchen schreibt schön.   The girl writes *beautifully*.

The Comparison of the Adverb

schön	schöner	am schönsten
beautifully	more beautifully	most beautifully

There is another absolute form, aufs beste:

Sie sang aufs beste.   She sang as best she could.

Four irregular adverbs are worth learning here:

	Positive	Comparative	Superlative
soon	bald	eher or früher	am ehesten
willingly	gern	lieber	am liebsten
much	viel	mehr	am meisten
little	wenig	weniger / minder	am wenigsten / am mindesten

Vocabulary

die Erde, earth
die Themse, Thames
das Gold, gold
das Eisen, iron
die Luft, air
der Elefant, elephant
der Schmetterling, butterfly
die Schwalbe, swallow
der Eiffelturm, Eiffel Tower
der Dom, cathedral
scharf, sharp
*aussehen, to look
wieviel? how much?

schnell, quick, fast
süss, sweet, sweetly
vorsichtig, careful(ly)
glücklich, happy, fortunate
tief, deep
komisch, funny
nett, nice (persons)
fleissig, industrious(ly)
faul, lazy
angenehm, pleasant
unangenehm, unpleasant
*vorkommen, to seem
kosten, to cost

Exercise 55

From the following " skeletons " make up comparisons, thus:

Die Maus, klein, der Hund.
Die Maus ist kleiner als der Hund.

London, gross, die Vereinigten Staaten. Die Erde, klein, die Sonne. Die Themse, lang, der Rhein. Paris, alt, Rom. Das Gold, hart, das Eisen. Die Stadt, gross, das Dorf. Die Luft, schwer, das Wasser. Der Elefant, stark, der Mann. Die Katze, falsch, der Hund. Der Knabe, klug, das Mädchen. Der Schmetterling, schnell, die Schwalbe. Die See, tief, der See. Der Eiffelturm, hoch, der Kölner Dom.

Exercise 56

Wieviel kosten diese Äpfel? Sind diese Kirschen teurer als jene dort? Diese sind am teuersten. Marie ist das netteste Mädchen im Dorf. Ottilie singt schön, Hilde singt schöner, aber Else singt am schönsten. Welcher Junge ist am klügsten? Otto ist der klügste, aber Konrad ist fast ebenso klug. Ist Belgien nicht so gross wie Holland? Dieses Mädchen ist ebenso hübsch wie ihre [1] Schwester. Je älter ein Mann wird, desto weniger kann er lernen. Ein höherer Baum als jener ist in unserem Garten. Können Sie Deutsch sprechen? Ja? Um so besser. Je früher wir ankommen, desto länger werden wir warten müssen. Je mehr er trank, desto durstiger wurde er. Diese Fahrräder sind am besten. Otto ist der grösste Junge in der Klasse. Es ist angenehmer hier im Garten als im Hause. Irmgard ist fleissiger als ihr Bruder. Wir müssen vorsichtiger durch diesen Nebel fahren. Diese Kirschen sind die süssesten. Der Garten sieht im Sommer hübscher aus als im Winter.

[1] Grammatically, seine should be used, but ihre is more common with das Mädchen and das Fräulein.

Exercise 57

The more industriously he works, the less he learns.
The water is colder to-day than yesterday.   It is getting
(werden) darker.   It was getting slowly lighter (brighter).
Otto is tall, Konrad is taller, and Wilhelm is the tallest.
Marie sings more sweetly than her sister.   Are you as
lazy as your brother?   This boy does not look as clever
as his brother.   The longer we wait here the darker
it will be when we go back home.   I have very little,
she has less and her cousin (girl) has least.   This dog
is the most faithful.   Is that knife sharper than this?
I answered as best I could.   I shall buy the biggest and
sweetest apples.   The teacher will give this book to the
cleverest schoolboy.

LESSON XXI

POSSESSIVE AND CORRELATIVE PRONOUNS

In old-fashioned English we could say *mine* host, *mine*
inn, *mine* enemy, but now we always say *my*.   *My*, *thy*,
our, *their*, *her*, *your*, always demand a noun to follow
them, while *mine*, *thine*, *ours*, *theirs*, *hers*, *yours*, can do
without a noun, but insist upon having a verb.   *My* book,
but the book is *mine*; *your* house, but this house is *yours*.

When the possessive is used as a pronoun it can be
represented in two ways:

1. By—

Singular			Plural
meiner (m)	meine (f)	meines (n)	meine (all genders)

These forms are treated exactly like ordinary adjectives
used without any article.

> Dein Vater ist arm, meiner ist reich.   Thy father is poor,
> mine is rich.
> Das ist nicht sein Buch, es ist meines.   That is not his book,
> it is mine.

2. By using the following form with the definite article:

Singular			Plural	
All genders			All genders	
(der, die or das) meinige	mine	(die)	meinigen
,, ,, deinige	thine	,,	deinigen
,, ,, seinige	his *or* its	,,	seinigen
,, ,, ihrige	hers *or* its	,,	ihrigen
,, ,, unsrige	ours	,,	unsrigen
,, ,, eurige	yours	,,	eurigen
,, ,, Ihrige	yours	,,	Ihrigen
,, ,, ihrige	theirs	,,	ihrigen

The above is the form that is used in comparisons. You will gather its meaning from the following examples:

> Ihr Haus ist älter als das unsrige. Your house is older than ours.
> Mein Freund ist ebenso arm wie der seinige. My friend is as poor as his.
> Unsere Strasse ist nicht so breit wie die ihrige. Our street is not so wide as theirs.
> Ihre Zähne sind schärfer als die meinigen. Your teeth are sharper than mine.
> Zu meinem Vater und dem seinigen. To my father and his.

From this last example it is clear that meinige and the rest are used just like ordinary adjectives with the definite article:

> In unserer Stadt und in der Ihrigen. In our city and in yours.

Derjenige means *that* or *the one*, and may either go with a noun or stand alone. This is how it is declined; it is always written as one word:

	Singular		Plural
Masculine	Feminine	Neuter	All genders
derjenige	diejenige	dasjenige	diejenigen
denjenigen	diejenige	dasjenige	diejenigen
desjenigen	derjenigen	desjenigen	derjenigen
demjenigen	derjenigen	demjenigen	denjenigen

Diejenigen, welche = those who (such as).

He who has come is not my friend = derjenige, welcher gekommen ist, ist nicht mein Freund.

(Instead of derjenige, welcher the one word wer may be used if no particular person is indicated. Wer das sagt, lügt! Who (or He who) says that, is lying!)

I have seen your house and your father's. Ich habe Ihr Haus und das (or dasjenige) Ihres Vaters gesehen.

Note that instead of derjenige, etc., der, die, das; pl. die, may be used.

derselbe   dieselbe   dasselbe   dieselben

This word means *the same*, and can be used, just like derjenige, as either an adjective or a pronoun.

Derselbe Mann, the same man. Derselbe, the same one.

Exercise 58

Diese Handschuhe sind meine, jene sind deine. Lesen Sie immer dieselbe Zeitung? Mein Haus ist nicht so gross wie das Ihrige. Ihr Garten ist länger als der unsrige. Ich habe mein Buch und das meines Bruders gelesen. Ich habe sein Auto gesehen, aber nicht das ihrige. Diejenigen, welche zu spät ankommen, müssen hier warten. Wir essen immer in demselben Restaurant. Er hat immer in derselben Strasse gewohnt. Wer nicht arbeitet, soll nicht essen. Sie hat meinen Hut gefunden, aber nicht den seinigen.

Exercise 59

These (das) are your books, not mine. His brother is cleverer than hers. My knife is sharper than yours (du *form*). Both aunts live in the same town. He is reading the same book. Those who do not work hard (= industriously) will learn nothing. Their trees are taller than ours. She always buys the same sweets. Our city is bigger than yours. His work is better than his sister's. His house is not so small as his uncle's. Those who work best may go home early.

LESSON XXII
ORDER OF WORDS

It is now worth while revising all that has been said about the order of words in German. You have now had experience of the order actually used, and so will be ready to appreciate general rules in a way you could not before.

Then shrieked the timid and stood still the brave. Here we have two independent clauses joined by *and*. Each could stand alone and make complete sense—*then the timid shrieked* is one statement, and *the brave stood still* is another. Such clauses are called principal or independent clauses.

The timid shrieked because the ship was sinking. Here *the timid shrieked* can stand alone as before and lead to no question. But we cannot read the clause *because the ship was sinking* without knowing that something important has been left out. The second clause, in fact, depends upon the first and is called a dependent or subordinate clause. In the following sentences the principal clause is printed in ordinary type, the subordinate or dependent clause in italics: He said *that he was poor.* The boys *who came this morning* have returned. Go *where he sends you.*

Examining these clauses we find that the words *that he was poor* tell us something. If we ask what he said the answer is *that he was poor.* This clause therefore stands for a thing and in fact does the duty of a noun, and is called a *noun clause.* *Who came this morning* tells us something about the boys, distinguishes these boys from other boys—in fact, it does the work of an adjective, and is called an *adjectival clause.* *Where he sends you* in like manner does the work of an adverb, and is called an *adverbial clause.*

Taking up the principal clause first, we find that, with two important exceptions, the order of words in German is the same as in English *if the sentence begins with the subject.* The two exceptions are:

1. The Past Participle, the Infinitive, and the Separable Prefix are always placed at the end of the clause, and if there be both a Past Participle and an Infinitive, the Infinitive goes to the end and the Past Participle takes the place second from the end. *Ich habe das Buch gekauft* = I have bought the book; *ich werde das Buch kaufen* = I shall buy the book; *ich kam nach Haus zurück* = I came back home; *ich werde geliebt werden* = I shall be loved.

2. The second exception is of the utmost importance to us, because we are very liable to make mistakes by carrying our English custom into German. In English we often put an adverb between the subject and the predicate—in fact, the very words we have just used illustrate this: we *often* put, etc. Now, this is never done in German. *We often put*, etc., must read wir setzen oft, etc. No word connected with the predicate can ever come between the subject and the personal verb. There are a few conjunctions which may be placed between the subject and the personal verb; the most usual of these are:

aber, but	nämlich, namely	jedoch, yet, still,
also, so, thus	indessen, whilst, however	however

as:

> Der König aber schlug ihn tot.   But the king struck him
>   dead.

You must be continually on your guard against putting in *adverbs* between the subject and its verb.

If for any reason the subject does not begin the clause, a peculiar change called *inversion* takes place, by which the subject is put *after* its personal verb. In English we might say, *The soldier fortunately was present*. This must be translated either: (1) Der Soldat war glücklicherweise zugegen, or (2) Glücklicherweise war der Soldat zugegen.

There are a few little words so insignificant that

they may come before the subject without causing inversion. These are:

aber, but	entweder, either	und, and
denn, for	oder, or	

So far we have been dealing with the principal clause. In the case of the *subordinate clause* the essential point is that the verb is placed at the end:

> Der Junge ging ins Bett, weil er krank war.   The boy went to bed because he was ill.
> Die Jungen, die heute morgen kamen, sind im Garten.   The boys who came this morning are in the garden.
> Gehen Sie, wohin er Sie schickt.   Go where he sends you.

In subordinate clauses the Separable Prefix joins up with its verb:

> Bevor er ausging, before he went out.

If two infinitives stand at the end, the auxiliaries haben, sein or werden will precede the infinitives instead of following:

> Da wir ihn haben finden können, as we have been able to find him.

In all sorts of clauses the following general principles are true:

1. Certain verbs govern two cases, one of which is the accusative, and the other may be either the genitive or the dative. The general rule of order in such cases is that of two nouns the dative comes before the accusative, the genitive after.

> Sie werden den König eines Unrechts anklagen.   They will accuse the king of an injustice.
> Schicken Sie dem Wirte die Briefe.   Send the letters to the landlord.

2. A personal pronoun, which is the object (whether direct or indirect) of the verb, generally comes before any noun or adverb in the clause.

> Er hat ihnen endlich die Briefe geschickt.   He has at last sent them the letters.

3. If there are several adverbs, they are usually arranged in the following order: (1) adverbs of *time*, (2) adverbs of *place*, (3) adverbs of *manner*.

Er hat es zuletzt gut getan.   He has done it well at last.
Wir haben morgens im Hause schwer gearbeitet.   We worked hard at home in the morning.

Vocabulary

der Strand, beach
der Kieselstein, pebble
der Sand, sand
die Garnele, shrimp
der Felsen, rock
die Klippen, cliffs
der Leuchtturm, lighthouse
der Krebs, crab
der Dampfer, steamer
das Segelschiff, sailing-boat
das Fischerboot, fishing-boat
die Pension, boarding-house
das Hotel (—s, —s), hotel
der Liegestuhl, deck-chair
die Hütte, hut
die Strandkabine, bathing-hut
der Badende, bather
die Ferien, holidays
die Kapelle, orchestra, band
der Sonnenhut, sun-hat
die Welle, wave
*anziehen, to put on (clothes)
*ausziehen, to take off (clothes)
*liegen, to lie (down)
*sitzen, to sit, be seated
mieten, to hire
packen, to pack
Fussball spielen, to play football

zurückkehren, to return
die Promenade, promenade
das Segel, sail
das Netz, net
das Schwimmbad, bathing-pool
der Badeanzug, bathing-costume
das Sonnenbad, sun-bath
die Boje, buoy
der Spaziergang, walk
der Ausflug, outing, excursion
die Seemöwe, seagull
das Sandschloss, sand-castle
die Bademütze, bathing-cap
der Strandschuh, beach-shoe
*schwimmen, to swim
*verbringen, to spend (time)
*ausgeben, to spend (money)
klettern, to climb
tauchen, to dive
retten, to rescue
*ertrinken, to be drowned
viel Spass haben, to have a good time
Golf spielen, to play golf
Cricket spielen, to play cricket
der Spass, joke

die Südküste (Ost-, Nord-, West-), South, East, North, West Coast

Exercise 60

Letzten Sommer verbrachten wir unsere Sommerferien an der Nordküste Deutschlands. Wir packten

unsere Koffer und fuhren am 28. August nach Swinemünde ab. Das Wetter war prachtvoll während des
ganzen Monates, den wir dort verbrachten. Wir wohnten in einem grossen Hotel, das neben dem Strand war.

Jeden Morgen standen wir früh auf. Nach dem
Frühstück gingen wir zum Strand hinunter. Wir
trugen unsere Badeanzüge mit uns, und wenn das
Wetter warm war, zogen wir unsere Badeanzüge und
Bademützen an und schwammen in der See. Ich kann
nicht wie (like) ein Fisch schwimmen, doch (yet)
schwimme ich sehr gern. Einige kleine Kinder, deren
Eltern (parents) in Liegestühlen sassen, machten Sand-
schlösser. Andere spielten Fussball oder suchten Gar-
nelen und Krebse mit ihren Netzen. Nach dem Baden
lagen wir auf dem warmen Sand und nahmen ein Sonnenbad. Bald wurden wir ganz braun, fast wie Neger
(black men). Eines Tages sahen wir einen Jungen in
der See. Er konnte nicht sehr gut schwimmen. Ein
Fischer hat ihn vom Ertrinken gerettet.

Manchmal machten wir einen Ausflug auf einem
Fischerboot. Das war sehr schön, und wir hatten viel
Spass. Wir tauchten von dem Boot in die See. Es
war ganz schön, wenn die Wellen gross waren. Oft
kletterten wir die Klippen hinauf, oder machten einen
Spaziergang den Strand entlang.[1]

Mein Vater hatte eine Strandkabine gemietet und so
konnten wir nachmittags Kaffee am Strand trinken.
Mein Vater spielte oft Golf auf dem schönen Golfplatz.
Wir waren ganz traurig, als wir nach Hause haben
zurückkehren müssen.

Exercise 61

I want to leave for Stuttgart to-morrow morning.
In the autumn we must pick the apples and plough the
fields. Where is the basket into which I put the apples?

[1] Entlang usually follows the noun in the accusative : *along
the beach.*

At Christmas we have four days holidays. We must not smoke here, for it is forbidden. The child whose parents are dead is very clever. I cannot read this letter because it is so badly written. Therefore you must show me the letter you wrote this morning. Yesterday it rained as I was coming up the street. The man to whom I was talking yesterday is the mayor. Before you go out show me the newspaper you bought this morning. He went out yesterday evening although he was ill. As it was so late he went immediately to bed. Whilst he was putting on his coat he heard somebody at the door.

LESSON XXIII

PASSIVE VOICE

The Imperfect of werden is very easy:

Imperfect of werden

Singular	Plural
1. ich wurde	wir wurden
2. du wurdest	Sie wurden
	ihr wurdet
3. er wurde	sie wurden

We can use werden with the Past Participle as well as with the Infinitive, but then it has quite a different meaning.

Ich werde lieben = I shall love.
Ich werde geliebt = I am loved.

Werden and the Infinitive make the Future tense; werden and the Past Participle make what is called the Passive voice. The Passive indicates that the subject of the verb does not act, but is rather acted upon. It indicates how the subject is affected by the action of others upon it.

The four commonest tenses of the Passive are: the Present, *I am loved*; the Imperfect, *I was loved*; the Perfect, *I have been loved*; and the Pluperfect, *I had been loved*.

Present: ich werde geliebt.
Imperfect: ich wurde geliebt.

To make the two Perfect tenses we require the Past Participle of werden. This Past Participle is geworden. Note that this Past Participle has no ge before it when it is used to form the Passive of another verb.

> Ich bin geworden means " I have become."
> Ich war geworden means " I had become."

So if we put in the Past Participle of lieben we get:

> Ich bin geliebt worden, meaning " I have become loved," or, more simply, " I have been loved."
> Ich war geliebt worden, means " I had become loved " or " I had been loved."

Sometimes the Past Participle is used like an adjective, and when this is done there is apt to be some confusion with the Passive. If we find a soldier lying dead with a bullet hole in his head we may say: Er ist getötet = he is killed. Here there is no action, therefore no Passive voice. Er wird getötet is the Passive form, and implies that he is being killed: that the killing is going on. When you are in doubt whether a Participle is to be used as a Passive or not, ask yourself whether you can put this action into the progressive form. Bestrafen = to punish. *I am punished.* Is the punishing going on? Yes; then ich werde bestraft. No; then ich bin bestraft. The following examples will help to make this point clear.

> I shall punish. Ich werde bestrafen.
> The soldiers are being rescued. Die Soldaten werden gerettet.
> The soldiers were rescued (*i.e.* were in the state of now being safe). Die Soldaten waren gerettet.

They had been rescued.   Sie waren gerettet worden.
I have been punished.   Ich bin bestraft worden.
She is asked.   Sie wird gefragt.

When *by* is used with the Passive it is always rendered von to denote the *agent*, durch to denote the *instrument*:

Der Knabe wird *von* seinem Vater bestraft.   The boy is punished by his father.
Der Soldat wurde *durch* einen Pfeil getötet.   The soldier was killed by an arrow.

Exercise 62

Put in the proper form of sein or werden (to form either Passive or Future) according to the meaning:

Dieser Briefkasten — dreimal am Tage (a day) vom Briefträger geleert (emptied). Dieser Brief — gestern von meiner Stenotypistin geschrieben. — der Brief schon geschrieben? Ich — meinen Freund in Bonn besuchen. Das Telegramm — gestern geschickt. Als wir ankamen, — die Tür schon geschlossen. Das Haus — schon gebaut worden. Dieses Kleid — letztes Jahr vom Schneider gemacht.

Exercise 63

I have been asked by my brother to [1] go to Berlin. These apples were picked yesterday by the baker's children. When (wann) will these letters be written? The child has been punished. This newspaper is read every day by thousands of (Tausenden von) men and women. Has the car already been repaired? Have you been seen by anyone? The letter-box is now being cleared (emptied) by the postman. This dress will be made by the tailor. When was this book written?

[1] Zu.   Do not forget that the infinitive goes to the end.

LESSON XXIV

GOVERNMENT OF VERBS

I. Verbs taking the Dative

As we have seen before, there are certain verbs which sometimes require *to* in English when the Dative without preposition is required in German. Such verbs take two objects, a direct and an indirect, this preceding the direct if both are nouns, and following if both are pronouns. If one is a pronoun and the other a noun, the pronoun comes first. Such are:

sich nähern, to approach	*(an)bieten, to offer
*geben, to give	widmen, to dedicate, devote
schenken, to present	*schreiben, to write [1]
reichen, to pass	sagen, to tell [2]
schicken, to send	erzählen, to relate, tell
erwidern, to reply	*leihen, to lend
zeigen, to show	*vorlesen, to read (aloud) to
*beschreiben, to describe	verweigern ⎱
*befehlen, to order	*abschlagen ⎰ to refuse
erlauben ⎱ to allow	vertrauen, to trust
gestatten ⎰	anvertrauen, to entrust

Examples:

Ich näherte mich dem Löwen. I drew near to the lion.
Er vertraute seinem Bruder das Kind an. He entrusted the child to his brother.
Wir schlugen es ihm ab. We refused it him.

The following govern the Dative, where the reason is not so apparent to the English student:

danken, to thank	dienen, to serve
antworten, to answer (person)	folgen, to follow
begegnen, to meet	*gefallen, to please
gehorchen, to obey	gehören, to belong
*geschehen, to happen	glauben, to believe (person)
*helfen, to help	nützen, to be of use
passen, to fit	schmeicheln, to flatter

---

[1] Also an + Acc. before noun. [2] To say to = sagen zu.

2. Verbs governing the Genitive

The Genitive noun *follows* the Accusative.

sich bedienen, to use
sich schämen,[2] to be ashamed of
berauben, to rob of
versichern, to assure of

sich erinnern,[1] to remember
anklagen, to accuse of
überzeugen, to convince of

3. Verbs followed by the Nominative

*bleiben, to remain
*heissen, to be called

*sein, to be
*werden, to become

4. Verbs taking a different Preposition

All the following verbs taking a preposition different from that in English take the Accusative, except those marked with a dagger (†), and these require the Dative.

(a) An:

adressieren, to address (message)
*denken, to think of
*sterben, to die of (illness) (†)
*sich wenden, to apply to
zweifeln, to doubt of (†)

glauben, to believe
sich lehnen, to lean against
erinnern, to remind of
sich erinnern, to remember
*teilnehmen, to take part in (†)

(b) Auf:

*achtgeben auf, pay attention to
antworten auf, answer (thing)
zählen auf, to count on

warten auf, to wait for
*sich verlassen auf, to rely on

(c) Aus:

*werden, to become (†)
*bestehen, to consist of (†)

übersetzen, to translate from (†)
machen, to make from (†)

(d) Bei:

*bleiben, to stay with (†)

wohnen, to live with (†)

---

[1] Also takes an + Acc.   [2] Also takes über + Acc.

(e) Nach:

fragen, to ask for (†)
zielen, to aim at (†)

schicken, to send for (†)
sich sehnen, to long for (†)

(f) Über:

sich ärgern, to be annoyed at
erstaunen, to be surprised at
sich wundern, to wonder at
sich freuen, to rejoice at
sich schämen, to be ashamed of

lachen, to laugh at [1]
spotten, to make fun of
erröten, to blush at
sich aufregen, to get excited at

(g) Um:

spielen, to play for
*bitten, to ask for

kämpfen, to struggle for

(h) Vor:

sich fürchten,[2] to be afraid of (†)
zittern, to tremble with (†)

warnen, to warn of (†)
schützen, to protect from (†)

Note also: vor Freude tanzen, to dance for joy
vor Hunger sterben, to die of hunger

Exercise 64

Ich dankte ihm für seinen Brief. Er starb an Gicht (gout). Er ärgerte sich über meine Antwort. Ich fragte nach dem Preis (price) der Äpfel. Er hat dieses Buch aus dem Deutschen übersetzt, während er bei seiner Tante wohnte. Er befahl dem Manne, auf den Zug zu warten. Das Mädchen errötete über diese Antwort. Ich vertraue Ihnen diese Arbeit an. Wem gehört das Haus mit dem roten Dach? Erlauben Sie mir, Ihnen zu helfen. Ich las meiner Mutter den Brief vor. Beschreiben Sie mir die Stadt, wo Sie wohnen. Erinnern Sie sich an den Tag, wo [3] wir dem Manne begegneten? Was ist aus Ihrem Bruder geworden? Der Junge lehnte

---

[1] But : I laugh at him. Ich lache ihn aus.
[2] I fear that . . . = ich fürchte, dass . . .
[3] When after a noun of time = wo.

sich an die Wand. Folgen Sie mir, bitte! Gefällt es Ihnen hier in England? Das englische Wetter gefällt mir nicht. Sie können sich auf ihn verlassen. Wann haben Sie Ihrer Schwester diese Armbanduhr geschenkt? Die anderen lachten und spotteten über den armen Jungen. Das kleine Mädchen fürchtete sich vor der grossen Kuh. Der arme Mann bat mich um Geld (money). Wir zitterten vor Kälte (cold).

Exercise 65

The girls and boys danced for joy. My nephew has become a sailor. I was surprised at his letter. Whom are you thinking of ? Ask for the price of the coat in the shop-window. Pass the sugar to your brother, please. Did you like the film yesterday evening? I do not believe her. Have you not sent for the doctor? I fear that we shall have bad weather to-morrow. I allowed the children to play in the garden. We told the policeman the whole story (die Geschichte). He asked me for money, but I refused it him. I do not remember the girl. He got excited at my answer, and ordered me to show him the book. He leaned against the door and would not allow me to go out. Are you afraid of lions? There is the man whom we met at the " Red Lion."

LESSON XXV

THE ENGLISH PRESENT PARTICIPLE

The English Present Participle of the verb (*i.e.* the part ending in -*ing*) is a fruitful source of difficulty to the English student of German. Here is a list of the main points to be noticed:

1. The German Present Participle in -end is used as an adjective before the noun (rarely can it be used after

it), and it may be used adverbially or to form a noun which in English would end in -*er*:

> Der sterbende Mann,[1] the dying man.
> Sie hat eine auffallend musikalische Stimme. She has a strikingly musical voice.
> Der Reisende,[2] der Badende, the traveller, the bather.

2. After the verb bleiben, *to remain*, and those mentioned in the next lesson, under the Infinitive, section 1 (c), the English Present Participle is rendered by the simple Infinitive:

> Er blieb sitzen. He remained sitting.
> Ich sah ihn spielen. I saw him playing.

3. When the English Present Participle is a noun the simple Infinitive is used in German:

> Das Rauchen ist hier verboten. Smoking is forbidden here.
> Er ist des Wartens müde. He is tired of waiting.

(Note the position of müde: adjectives in German frequently come at the end like this.)

4. In most other cases it is best to turn the Present Participle into a clause, co-ordinate with und, subordinate or relative, according to the meaning. Note the following:

> He sat smoking on a chair = he sat on a chair and smoked.
> The girl wearing the green dress = the girl who wears a green dress.
> On opening the window = when I opened.
> Before going out = before I went out.
> Knowing he was ill = as I knew he was ill.
> " Yes," he said, putting on his coat = whilst he put on his coat.

---

[1] But we cannot say: Der Mann ist sterbend. We can say: Das Mädchen ist reizend, *the girl is charming*, because reizend is purely adjectival, whereas sterbend is verbal in force.

[2] Such nouns, and those formed from adjectives or Past Participles, are declined as though they were adjectives followed by a noun.

5. After kommen, *to come*, the Germans have a curious use of the Past Participle instead of the Present Participle to denote the mode of coming:

> Er kam gehüpft, gelaufen, gesprungen, gekrochen, he came hopping, running, jumping, crawling, etc.

Exercise 66

Bevor er ins Bett ging, schrieb er einen Brief. Nachdem er die Zeitung gelesen hatte, ging er aus. Indem er seinen Mantel anzog und seinen Hut aufsetzte, lief er aus dem Zimmer. Das Baden ist hier verboten. Er sass in dem Garten und rauchte eine Pfeife. Wer ist das Mädchen, das den grünen Hut trägt? Wir hörten unsere Kusine singen. Er blieb an der Tür stehen. Da ich wusste (knew),[1] dass er zu Hause war, telephonierte ich ihm. Als ich zum Fenster hinaussah, sah ich das Auto unseres Arztes vorbeifahren. Er sah sie Tennis spielen. Er rauchte, während er sich rasierte. Das kleine Mädchen kam gelaufen und sprach zu uns. Ich stand auf, als ich den Mann hereinkommen sah, aber meine Schwester blieb sitzen.

Exercise 67

Seeing the letter on the table I read it. " Are you ready? " he asked, putting on his coat. He stood near the door, reading a newspaper. The man was working and his wife was playing the piano. I asked him to sit [2] down, but he remained standing. On opening the drawer we found a letter from him. Who is the man riding the big black horse? We found them weeping. Before going out he 'phoned to his brother. Knowing it was late we decided not to visit our uncle. After seeing the advertisement in the paper he 'phoned to his sister.

---

[1] *Wissen, *to know* through the brain (*facts*).
*Kennen, *to know* by sight, hearing, touch, smell, taste.
[2] *To sit down* (take one's seat), sich setzen.
To sit, be sitting, be seated, *sitzen.

The dying sailor asked for water.   The man is dying.
Going along the street I met my dentist.   I used to
know this doctor.   He knows nothing.

LESSON XXVI

VERBS WITH SEIN—THE INFINITIVE

Up till now we have always used the verb haben to
make the Perfect or Pluperfect of a verb, as in ich habe
es getan = I have done it.   But there are a good many
verbs that require the verb sein instead of the verb
haben.   In English we can say either *I am come* or *I
have come*, but in German it *must* be ich bin gekommen.

Lists are sometimes given of verbs that take sein and
those that take haben, but these are very tiresome to
learn, and it is better if we can hit upon any way of dis-
covering *from the meaning* whether a verb should have
haben or sein.   It may be accepted as a rule that *all*
verbs having a direct object must use haben.   Of other
verbs, the sein class may be detected by applying the
following test: Is the action of the verb followed by a
corresponding state?   If it is, then use sein; if it is not,
use haben.   The question may be best put—If I have
done so-and-so, am I so-and-so?

For example: If I have come, am I come?   The answer
is clearly *yes*; so we use sein.   If I have died, am I dead?
Again *yes*; so we use sein.   Er ist gestorben = he has
died.   If I have fought, am I fought?   The answer is *no*;
so we write er hat gekämpft.

Some of the commonest verbs of the sein class are:

*bleiben, to remain, stay	reisen, to travel
eilen, to hasten	*gelingen, to succeed
*fliegen, to fly	*kommen, to come
*fallen, to fall	*steigen, to mount
*sein, to be	*werden, to become
*sinken, to sink	*wachsen, to grow
*gehen, to go	wandern, to wander

E

The Infinitive

1. The Infinitive *without* zu is used after

    (a) the verb werden,
    (b) the modal auxiliaries (müssen, können, etc.),
    (c) the following verbs:

*helfen, to help	fühlen, to feel
hören, to hear	lehren, to teach
*lassen, to cause	lernen, to learn
*sehen, to see	

We have already seen this in the case of werden and the Modal Auxiliaries. Here are examples of the others:

Ich sah sie spielen.	I saw her *playing*.
Sie lehrten mich singen.	They taught me to sing.
Ich lernte dort schwimmen.	I learnt to swim there.

The zu is also omitted in certain expressions:

Er geht schwimmen.	He is going swimming.
Er tut nichts als schlafen.	He does nothing but sleep.

2. In other cases zu is used before the Infinitive. Remember that zu comes between the Separable Prefix and the Infinitive, forming one word, but in other cases forms two words:

    Er bat mich, ihn zu begleiten.   He asked me to accompany him.
    Ich wünschte auszugehen.   I desired to go out.
    Ich versprach, früh nach Hause zu kommen.   I promised to come home early.
    Er befahl mir, nach Berlin zu reisen.   He ordered me to go to Berlin.
    Wir beschlossen in Bonn zu übernachten.   We decided to stay the night in Bonn.

The verb lassen

The verb lassen mentioned in Section 1 above is very important. It means *to have something done, to cause to be done, to get something done.* Like the Modal Auxiliaries, the Infinitive instead of the Past Participle is used after another Infinitive. Note these examples:

> Ich lasse mir die Haare schneiden. I have (am having) my hair cut.
> Ich liess mir die Haare schneiden. I had my hair cut.
> Ich habe mir die Haare schneiden lassen. I have had my hair cut.
> Ich werde mir die Haare schneiden lassen. I shall have my hair cut.
> Ich beschloss, mir die Haare schneiden zu lassen. I decided to have my hair cut.

Note 1. The English *Past Participle* in such cases is in German the *Infinitive*. *Cut* (Past Participle) becomes in German *to cut*. The exact meaning is: *I cause to cut.*

Note 2. In talking of parts of the *body* or *dress*, unless any misunderstanding might arise, the definite article is used instead of the possessive adjective (*my, his,* etc.). Possession is indicated by the Dative of the noun or pronoun:

> Ich liess mir die Haare schneiden. I had my hair cut.

This is true of constructions other than with lassen:

> Ich trat dem Manne auf den Fuss. I trod on the man's foot (*literally :* I trod to the man on the foot).
> Ich wusch mir die Hände. I washed my hands.
> But: Seine Hände waren furchtbar schmutzig. His hands were terribly dirty. (If die were used, possession would be vague and the sentence would be ridiculous.)

Exercise 68

Ich gehe heute nachmittag mit meinem Freund schwimmen. Hast du versprochen, ihm ein Buch zu schicken? Mein Onkel lehrte mich Klavier spielen. Ich lasse mir die Haare schneiden. Ich habe mir ein neues Haus bauen lassen. Wo haben Sie Golf spielen gelernt? Helfen Sie mir einsteigen! Müssen Sie jetzt nach Hause gehen? Wir werden uns in Paris neue

E 2

Kleider machen lassen. Er beschloss, mit dem Auto
nach Dresden zu fahren. Ich beschloss, mir die Haare
schneiden zu lassen. Mein Vater hat mir versprochen,
mich vom Bahnhof abzuholen. Wünschen Sie morgen
abzufahren? Ich befahl dem Kellner, mir eine Flasche
Wein zu bringen. Ich habe mir eine Flasche Wein
bringen lassen. Wir sahen ihn im Walde reiten.
Waschen Sie ihm die Hände! Hast du dir die Hände
gewaschen? Ich habe ihm die Hände gewaschen. Der
Frisör (barber) hat dem Manne die Haare geschnitten.
Schneiden Sie mir bitte die Haare nicht zu kurz! Hast
du dir die Fingernägel (finger-nails) gefärbt (tinted) und
die Augenbrauen rasiert (shaved = plucked)? Ich lasse
mir die Schuhe putzen (clean). Ist er nach Hause gegangen? Sie sind noch nicht angekommen. Mein
Bruder ist gestern nach Amsterdam geflogen.

Exercise 69

I heard you singing in the garden. Who taught you
to play the piano? Shall I buy you a few cigarettes
when I am in the town? We have hastened to the
station to meet you. Have you travelled in Russia?
The trees in your garden have grown very tall. I had
the grass of the lawn cut yesterday. I shall have a new
suit made next week. We have often wandered over
these fields. Have you stayed at home all day? Can
you get this wheel repaired for me? I have had a glass
of wine brought for you. Shall I have these things sent
(zuschicken) to you? I have decided to have my hair
waved (ondulieren). Will you teach me to dive? We
promised to send them a letter every week. He asked her
to write to him. Have you ordered the waiter to bring
some more bread? No, I have ordered [1] some cigarettes.
Do you wish to listen to the wireless?

---

[1] *To order* something, bestellen. *To order* a person to do
something, *befehlen.

LESSON XXVII

THE SUBJUNCTIVE

I. The Formation of the Subjunctive

The Present Tense

In learning the Subjunctive forms of the verbs the student must remember the " Subjunctive e." All the endings have e, as the following examples will show, and in the Present Tense this e is added in all cases to the stem of the verb, *i.e.* that part left after taking off -(e)n:

haben	lieben	müssen
hab-e	lieb-e	müss-e
hab-est	lieb-est	müss-est
hab-e	lieb-e	müss-e
hab-en	lieb-en	müss-en
hab-et	lieb-et	müss-et
hab-en	lieb-en	müss-en

The one exception to this is the verb sein:

sei	seien
seiest	seiet
sei	seien

You will note the ich sei and er sei have no e.

The Imperfect Tense

In the case of *Weak* Verbs there is nothing to learn, as their Imperfect Tense is exactly the same as the Indicative.

Strong Verbs form the Imperfect Subjunctive by adding the e endings given above to the stem of the Imperfect Indicative, which is modified when possible.

Infinitive	sein	haben	müssen	singen
Imperfect Ind.	war	hatte	musste	sang
Imperfect Subj.	wäre	hätte	müsste	sänge

2. Use of the Subjunctive

One of the most important uses of the Subjunctive is in *Indirect* or *Reported Speech*. Notice the following:

> *Direct Speech :* He said : " I *am* ill."
> *Indirect Speech :* He said he *was* ill.

In English the Present Tense (*am*) becomes Past Tense (*was*) in Indirect Speech. In German the Present Tense of Direct Speech should correctly become the Present Subjunctive, but many Germans use the Imperfect Subjunctive, especially in conversation:

> *Direct Speech :* Er sagte : " Ich bin krank."
> *Indirect Speech :* Er sagte, dass er krank sei (or wäre).

The dass in Indirect Speech may be omitted. Notice the word order:

> Er sagte, er sei (or wäre) krank.

The Present Subjunctive is *not* used if it has the same form as the Present Indicative. The Imperfect Subjunctive must be used in such a case. Let us compare the Present Subjunctive and Present Indicative of the verb haben :

Pres. Subj.	Pres. Ind.
ich habe	habe
habest	hast
habe	hat
wir haben	haben
habet	habt
sie haben	haben

Thus those forms which are the same in both moods are the ich, wir and sie forms, and they must be replaced by hätte, hätten. As, however, the Imperfect Subjunctive may be used in all cases, and usually is in conversational style, the student is advised to *keep to the Imperfect Subjunctive in Reported Speech*, until his command of the language is more complete.

If the tense of the actual words is *Past* in English, then the student should use the *Pluperfect* (although more correctly the Perfect, except when this is the same as the Perfect Indicative in form):

Direct : The policeman said : " I found the book."
Indirect : The policeman said he (had) found the book.

In German:

Direct : Der Schutzmann sagte : " Ich habe das Buch gefunden."
Indirect : Der Schutzmann sagte, dass er das Buch gefunden
hätte (sagte, er hätte das Buch gefunden).

General Rule for the Subjunctive in Indirect Speech

After a verb (in the Past Tense) of *saying, declaring, believing, asking,*[1] *answering, reporting, fearing, thinking, relating, suspecting, surmising,* etc., the Subjunctive must be used in the following clause as explained above.

Another use of the Subjunctive is the 3rd Person Imperative form (see also p. 90):

Er gehe nach Hause !
or : Er soll nach Hause gehen }Let him go home.
or : Lasst ihn nach Hause gehen !

Notice also the exclamatory wish:

Es lebe der König ! }Long live the King !
Hoch lebe der König !

Vocabulary

der Salon, drawing-room	das Wohnzimmer, living-room
der Schlüssel, key	die Elektrizität, electricity
der Stock (das Stockwerk), storey, floor	das Feuer, fire
	der Boden, floor
der Aufzug, lift	der Teppich, carpet
der Heizkörper, radiator	der Spiegel, mirror
die Zentralheizung, central heating	der Kamin, mantelpiece, English fireplace

[1] Fragen, *to ask*, takes ob, *whether, if*, which, unlike dass, may never be omitted.

der Ofen, German stove [1]
der Vorhang, curtain
der Wecker, alarm-clock
der Kleiderständer, coat-rack
der Schirmständer, umbrella-stand
der Rollvorhang, blind
*hinaufgehen, to go up
*hinunterlaufen, to run down
anknipsen, fo switch on
aufwachen, to wake up
modern,[2] modern, up-to-date
schuldig, owing
das Gas, gas
das Studierzimmer, study
die Garage, garage
das Schlafzimmer, bedroom
das Badezimmer, bathroom
die Treppe, stairs
der Schornstein, chimney

*bekommen } to get, obtain, re-
kriegen } ceive
*schliessen, to lock
*herunterlassen, to let down
hängen, to hang
*heraufziehen, to pull up
beleuchtet, lighted
klingeln (nach), to ring (for)
bedecken, to cover
sich wärmen, to warm oneself
ausmachen, to put out
wecken, to wake (someone)
*hinauffahren, to go up (in a lift)
die Mark (no pl.), mark
sicher, certain(ly)
die Nummer, number
bitte sehr ! not at all !
was für, what sort of
*vergessen, to forget

Exercise 70

Chauffeur, fahren Sie zu einem modernen aber billigen Hotel. Ich will in dieser Stadt einige Wochen verbringen. Hier ist ein gutes Hotel, mein Herr : der Riesenfürstenhof. Gut! Ich steige hier aus. Wieviel bin ich Ihnen schuldig? Drei Mark fünfzig? Hier ist Trinkgeld für Sie. Danke schön, mein Herr! Bitte sehr! Kann ich ein Zimmer für einige Nächte bekommen? Ja, sicher! Was für eines? Ich will nicht zu viel ausgeben.

Der Mann sagte, er hätte einige schöne Zimmer, die ganz ruhig und hell beleuchtet wären. Ich antwortete, dass ich sie ansehen möchte. Er sagte, ich könnte mit dem Aufzug hinauffahren: Nummer 15. Ich fragte, wo der Aufzug wäre. Er erwiderte, dass er in der Ecke wäre. Ich fragte den Liftjungen, ob das Hotel Zentralheizung hätte. " Ja, sicher! " antwortete er. Er fragte, zu welchem Zimmer ich ginge. Ich sagte, dass ich dort einige Tage verbringen würde. Ich fragte, ob das

---

[1] A stove for heating purposes which replaces the English open fireplace.   [2] Pron. mo-dern'.

Hotel eine Garage hätte? Ob das Hotel in allen Zimmern durch Elektrizität beleuchtet wäre? Er sagte mir, dass ein Badezimmer neben meinem Zimmer wäre, und dass Zentralheizung in allen Zimmern wäre.

Ich klingelte nach dem Portier. Ich fragte ihn, ob er mich um 5 Uhr wecken würde. Er antwortete, dass er es nicht vergessen würde. Ich zog den Rollvorhang herauf und sah auf die Strasse hinunter.

Exercise 71

The driver said he was quite ready. I asked him if he knew (wissen or kennen?) where the Hotel Bismarck was. He said he had never seen it. I asked the policeman whether the post office was in that street. She said he was coming on Monday. The girl said she had seen his car in the garage. The man told me she had gone by air to England. I replied that I had missed the train. She asked me if I would like to play with them. Long live our friends from Germany!

LESSON XXVIII

THE CONDITIONAL SENTENCE

The so-called Conditional tense or mood is formed with the Imperfect Subjunctive of werden + the Infinitive.

ich würde gehen	I should [1] go
du würdest gehen	you would [2] go
er würde gehen	he would go
wir würden gehen	we should go
ihr würdet gehen	you would go
sie würden gehen	they would go
Sie würden gehen	you would go

---

[1] The English *should* also means *ought to* : we shall deal with this later in this lesson.

[2] The English *would* also means *wanted to* and *used to* :

He would not answer. Er wollte nicht antworten.

He would often go out in the evenings. Er ging oft abends aus (oft ging er abends aus).

The above tense, as we prefer to call it, is used when an *if* is expressed or understood, and to translate *should* or *would* in Indirect Speech:

> Ich würde das Haus kaufen, wenn es billiger wäre. I should buy the house if it were cheaper.
>
> Er sagte, dass sie kommen würde. He said she would be coming.

The *If* Clause

As will be seen above, wenn, *if*, is followed by the Imperfect Subjunctive to express a hypothesis or condition impossible or unlikely to be fulfilled.

> Wenn ich das Geld hätte. If I had the money.
>
> Wenn er nach Hause käme. If he came (were to come) home.

The wenn, like the *if* in English, may be omitted:

> Hätte ich das Geld. Had I the money (= if I had).

The würde clause may be replaced by the Imperfect Subjunctive, while the Pluperfect Subjunctive is much to be preferred to the Second or Perfect Conditional. This subjunctive construction in both Simple and Second Conditional must be used in the case of the Modal Auxiliaries, as set out on page 139. Consider the following examples:

1. SIMPLE CONDITIONAL: *If he were here I would show it to him* may be translated:

> (i) Wenn er hier wäre, würde ich es ihm zeigen, or
>
> (ii) Wäre er hier, zeigte ich es ihm, or
>
> (iii) Wenn er hier wäre, zeigte ich es ihm, or
>
> (iv) Wäre er hier, würde ich es ihm zeigen.

Or the second clause may be put first. Of the above perhaps it is best for the student to keep to the first.

2. SECOND CONDITIONAL: *If he had been here I would have shown it to him* may be translated:

> (i) Wenn er hier gewesen wäre (Wäre er hier gewesen), hätte ich es ihm gezeigt.
>
> (ii) Wenn er hier gewesen wäre (Wäre er hier gewesen), würde ich es ihm gezeigt haben.

Of these two the student had better keep to the former, that being the more usual.

The Modal Auxiliaries

We have said before that the Imperfect Subjunctive of the modal auxiliaries is used instead of the Simple Conditional with würde, and the Pluperfect Subjunctive instead of the Second Conditional:

Simple Conditional:

> Ich könnte nicht gehen.   I could not (should not be able to) go.
> Ich müsste Deutsch lernen.   I should have to learn German.
> Ich möchte diesen Film sehen.   I should like to see this film.
> Ich sollte nach Hause gehen.   I should (ought to) go home.

Second Conditional:

> Ich hätte nicht gehen können.   I could not have gone (should not have been able to go).
> Ich hätte Deutsch lernen müssen.   I should have had to learn German.
> Ich hätte gerne diesen Film gesehen.   I should have liked to see this film (preferable to the construction with mögen).
> Ich hätte nach Hause gehen sollen.   I should (ought to) have gone home.

Als ob, als wenn, as though, as if

If followed by a Past tense als ob and als wenn are followed by a *past subjunctive*:

> Er sieht aus, als ob er ein Gespenst gesehen hätte.   He looks as though he had seen a ghost.

Exercise 72

If you had the money would you like to go to the United States?   If I were you I should go home at once (gleich). Had my friend been at home I should have spent the night with him.   She would have missed the train if she had not gone to the station by taxi. I should have telephoned you had I not been able to come. I told them I would help them if I could. I should have liked to go with you to the theatre, but I was terribly busy. If the lift had been in order I should not have fallen (fallen) down the stairs. I asked him how much I owed him. He asked me if I was getting out there. I asked him if he could switch on the light. He asked me if I desired to go up by the lift. I told him I got a letter from her every week. The driver asked me to what sort of hotel I would like to go. I told him I had come up the stairs. The liftboy said he put an alarm-clock on the mantelpiece of my room. The girl looked as though she had spent several weeks by the (an der) sea.

LESSON XXIX

REFLEXIVE VERBS

(i) When the action of a verb is reflected back to the subject the Reflexive Pronoun must be used, even after a preposition. The Reflexive Pronoun is Accusative if the direct object and Dative if indirect.

Accusative

ich wasche mich, I wash myself
*du wäschst dich, you wash yourself
er wäscht sich, he washes himself
sie wäscht sich, she washes herself
wir waschen uns, we wash ourselves
ihr wascht euch, you wash yourselves
sie waschen sich, they wash themselves
Sie waschen sich, you wash yourself (yourselves)

* Or : du wäschest.

Imperfect

ich wusch mich, I washed myself

Perfect

Ich habe mich gewaschen, I have washed myself

Dative

ich wasche mir die Hände, I wash my hands, etc.
du wäschst dir   ,,
er wäscht sich   ,,
sie wäscht sich   ,,
wir waschen uns   ,,
ihr wascht euch   ,,
sie waschen sich   ,,
Sie waschen sich   ,,

He looked behind him.	Er blickte hinter sich.
He spoke to himself.	Er sprach vor sich hin.
He has no money on him.	Er hat kein Geld bei sich.

(ii) In English *myself*, *himself*, etc., are frequently used, not reflexively, but to add force to the subject. In such cases selber or selbst must be used in German and placed after the direct object:

He did it himself.   Er tat es selbst.

(iii) In English we commonly use what is sometimes called a neuter verb to express a passive state when the agent is unknown or too unimportant in the mind of the speaker. In such cases the active reflexive verb is often used in German:

Suddenly the door opened.   Plötzlich öffnete sich die Tür.

(iv) Here is a list of verbs which are " neuter " in English and where the German reflexive is easily understood:

sich ändern, change (= vary)	sich rasieren, to shave
sich ankleiden, to dress	*sich waschen, to wash
sich auskleiden, to undress	sich regen, to stir, move
sich fühlen, to feel	sich rühren, to move (away)
sich lehnen, to lean	sich umdrehen, to turn round

(v) Here is a list of verbs where the German reflexive is not so apparent:

*sich befinden,[1] to be (found)	sich fragen, to wonder
sich bemühen, to endeavour	sich setzen, to sit down
*sich umsehen, to have a look round	sich weigern, to refuse
	sich verirren, to lose one's way
sich aufregen, to get excited	sich totlachen, to die of laughing
sich legen, to lie down	
sich irren, to be mistaken	sich erholen, to recover (health)
*sich betragen, to behave	
sich erkälten, to catch cold	*sich unterhalten, to converse
sich freuen, to be glad	sich beeilen, to hasten
sich erinnern,[2] to remember	sich bedienen,[3] to use

(vi) Verbs with the Dative Reflexive Pronoun:

*sich vornehmen, to propose, plan, arrange	sich vorstellen ⎫ to imagine sich einbilden ⎭
*sich wehtun, to hurt oneself	

(vii) The Reflexive Pronoun in the Dative is also often used as (a) the Dative of Advantage, and (b) to indicate possession where the article is used instead of the possessive adjective in talking of parts of the body or dress (see Lesson XXVI, under: The Verb lassen, page 130).

(a) Dative of Advantage:

Er liess sich ein Haus bauen.   He had a house built for himself.

Er kaufte sich einen Radioapparat.   He bought himself a wireless-set.

Ich sah mir die Schaufenster an.   I had a look at the shop-windows.

(b) In speaking of the body or dress:

Er schnitt sich in den Finger.   He cut his finger.

Er brach sich das Genick.   He broke his neck.

Ich liess mir die Haare schneiden.   I had my hair cut.

---

[1] Sich befinden = to be in health or be situated.

[2] Sich erinnern takes the Genitive or an with Acc.

[3] Sich bedienen takes the Genitive.

Vocabulary

der Wunsch, wish
von mir, of mine
sich erfüllen, to be fulfilled
abgesehen von, apart from
*wiedersehen, to see again
besonders, particularly
so viel, so much
die Schönheit, beauty
eigen, own
die Eisenbahn, railway
endlich, at last
mieten, to hire
das Schiff, ship
der Weg, way
nebst, together with
die Sperre, barrier
passieren, to pass
sorgfältig, carefully
prüfen, to examine
der Reisepass, passport
die Sache, thing, article
zollpflichtig, dutiable
verneinen, to say no
*vorbeilassen, to allow to pass
der Holzsteg, wooden gangway
gebräunt, sun-tanned
wetterhart, weather-beaten
der Zug, feature
*herumlaufen, to run about
das Gesicht, face
läuten, to ring, tinkle
sich schaukeln, to toss, pitch
der Schaum, foam
der Bug, bow (of ship)
die Einwanderung, immigration
der Offizier, officer
sich's bequem machen, to make oneself comfortable
seefest, a good sailor
*sinken, to sink
der Zollbeamte, Customs officer
sich ankleiden, to dress

bewundern, to admire
enttäuschen, to disappoint
der Reisemorgen, morning of the departure
*anbrechen, to break, dawn
der Wettergott, " clerk of the weather "
herabstrahlen, to shine down
die Fahrt, journey
das Deck, deck
bekannt, acquainted
die Reise, journey
vertraut, familiar
bequem, comfortable
seekrank, seasick
laut, loud
ohrenbetäubend, deafening
das Sirenengeheul, blast of the siren
anzeigen, to indicate
der Hafen, harbour
offen, open
gekräuselt, ruffled
malerisch, picturesque
der Eindruck, impression
immer ferner, further and further
rücken, to move
an etwas (Dat.) *vorbeifahren, to go past something
die Boje, buoy
der Westen, the west
*einfahren, to enter (vehicle)
aufspritzen, to splash up
plaudern, to converse
einander, one another
zu, to, for
der Inhalt, contents
untersuchen, to overhaul
neugeboren,[1] new-born
Gott sei Dank ! Thank Heaven !
sich auskleiden, to undress

---

[1] Ich fühle mich wie neugeboren, I feel like a giant refreshed.

Exercise 73
Eine Schiffahrt von Ostende nach Dover

Ein grosser Wunsch von mir sollte sich endlich erfüllen.
Meine Eltern versprachen, dass ich einen Freund in London
besuchen dürfte. Ganz abgesehen von dem Wiedersehen mit ihm (ich hatte ihn seit einem Jahre nicht mehr
gesehen), freute ich mich besonders auf die Seereise. Ich
hatte immer schon so viel von der Schönheit der See
gehört und gelesen, dass ich mich danach sehnte, diese
Schönheit mit meinen eignen Augen bewundern zu
dürfen. Ich wurde nicht enttäuscht. Der Reisemorgen
brach endlich an. Der Wettergott schien mir ganz
freundlich zu sein, und die Sonne strahlte hell vom
tiefblauen Himmel herab.

Nach einer langen Eisenbahnfahrt von Wiesbaden
kam ich um 4 Uhr in Ostende an. Ich mietete mir einen
Gepäckträger, meine Koffer auf das Schiff zu bringen.
Nebst allen anderen Reisenden passierte ich eine Sperre,
wo mein Reisepass sorgfältig geprüft wurde. Man fragte
mich, ob ich keine zollpflichtigen Sachen hätte. Ich
verneinte. Nachdem ich meine Koffer geöffnet hatte,
wurde ich vorbeigelassen. Ich ging über den Holzsteg
auf das grosse Schiff. Es war ein belgisches Schiff.
Ein paar Matrosen mit gebräuntem Gesicht und wetterharten Zügen liefen auf dem Deck herum. Ich sah mich
ein wenig auf dem Schiff um. Ich wurde bald mit einem
jungen Engländer bekannt, der diese Reise schon ein
paarmal gemacht hatte und ein bisschen vertrauter mit
allem war. Er zeigte mir, wo wir bequem sitzen könnten
und vor dem Wind gut geschützt wären. Ein lautes,
ohrenbetäubendes Sirenengeheul zeigte an, dass wir zum
Abfahren fertig waren. Wir fuhren aus dem Hafen in
die offene See.

Die bunten Segel der Fischerboote sahen im Sonnenschein sehr schön aus. Die See, von einem angenehm
frischen Wind ganz leicht gekräuselt, machte einen male-

rischen Eindruck. Ostende, mit seinem schönen Strand und den grossen Hotels rückte immer ferner und ferner.

Wir fuhren an den Bojen vorbei, die im Wasser läuteten und sich schaukelten. Nach drei Stunden Fahrt konnten wir die weisse Küste von England sehen. Eine Stunde später plauderten die Reisenden lustig miteinander und suchten ihre Koffer, um sich zum Aussteigen fertig zu machen. Das Schiff fuhr in den Hafen von Dover ein. Die Sonne sank schon langsam im Westen. In Dover prüften die Einwanderungsoffiziere unsere Reisepässe und die Zollbeamten untersuchten unsere Koffer. Ich stieg in ein Abteil des wartenden D-Zuges nach London und machte es mir bequem. Ich liess mir eine Tasse englischen Tee bringen. Dann fühlte ich mich wie neugeboren. Gott sei Dank! Ich war seefest gewesen!

Exercise 74

He is washing himself in the bathroom. She has already washed her hands. Have you any money on you? Did you repair the tyre yourself? The door opened and a tall man came in. She is dressing, I believe. I feel quite queer (komisch). Two boys were leaning against the door, conversing with one another. She turned quickly round. The Town Hall was in (the) Frederick Street (Friedrichstrasse). Not a leaf stirred. They sat down on the chair. Have you shaved? They quickly undressed. I am going to have a look round (in) the town. You are mistaken if you think (= believe) that I am a Frenchman. I have caught a cold. We have proposed to visit a few friends in Bonn. We lost our way in the wood. Do you remember the name (Der Name, des Namens) of our hotel? I am glad you have arrived. The child lay down on the bed and wept. Why (warum) are you getting so excited? My sisters are having a look at the shop windows. Wash yourself! Wash your hands! Do not turn round! Sit down, please! I have arranged to spend a few days in Dresden.

LESSON XXX

IMPERSONAL VERBS

We must now deal with a number of Impersonal Verbs, *i.e.* those with es, *it*, as their subject.

The translation of *There is, There are*

(i) *There is, there are (was, were)* are rendered by es ist (sind, war, waren) or by es gibt, es gab (no plural form). Es ist is used where the space is limited to a certain spot, es gibt when *there is* or *there are* refers to a wide or vague area. Compare the following:

> Es sind einige Kühe auf der Wiese. There are some cows in the field.
> Es gibt viele schöne Dörfer in diesem Lande. There are many beautiful villages in this country.
> Es ist kein Zucker übrig im Speiseschrank. There is no more sugar in the cupboard.
> Es gibt keine Gespenster. There are no ghosts.

Notice that es ist (sind) is followed by the Nominative, whereas es gibt takes the Accusative:

> Es war ein König. There was a king.
> Es gibt keinen Menschen, der unsterblich ist. There is no man who is immortal.

Notice further that *there was* (once upon a time) is always es war:

> Es waren einmal drei Prinzen. There were once three princes.

In inversion the es with sein is omitted, but not with geben:

> Einmal war ein Mann. Once there was a man.
> Plötzlich gab es einen lauten Krach. Suddenly there was a loud crash.

Es gibt may be used in other tenses:

> Es hat gegeben, there has (have) been.
> Es hatte gegeben, there had been.
> Es wird geben, there will be.
> Es würde geben, there would be.

There is (*are, was, were*) requires very careful thought in translating it into German. It is used so loosely and extensively in English that very often it is better to use another verb, like *stand, lie, hang, to take place, to find oneself* (sich befinden), etc. Note the following:

> Es standen zwei Männer an der Strassenecke. There were two men (standing) at the street-corner.
> Es lagen einige Bücher auf dem Tisch. There were a few books on the table.
> Es hingen einige Bilder an der Wand. There were some pictures on the wall.
> Es klopft jemand. There is somebody knocking.
> Es riefen und sangen Männer und Weiber auf der Strasse. There were men and women shouting and singing in the street.
> Ein grosses Fest fand in diesem Saale statt. There was a great feast in this hall.

The following verbs are always Impersonal:

> es schneit, it snows
> es regnet, it rains
> es blitzt, it lightens
> es ist windig, it is windy
> es ist Nacht, it is night

The following are only accidentally used impersonally:

> es wird dunkel, it is getting dark
> es klopft, there is a knock
> es zieht, there is a draught
> es wird erzählt, dass . . ., it is said that
> es wurde getanzt, there was dancing
> es wurde getrunken und gesungen, there was drinking and singing
> es wurde gepfiffen, a whistle went (was blown)

The following govern the Accusative:

es geht mich an, it concerns me
mich friert, I am freezing
es freut mich, I am glad
es wundert mich, I wonder
es ärgert (verdriesst) mich, it annoys me
es langweilt mich, it bores me

The following govern the Dative:

es kommt mir vor, it seems (appears) to me
es scheint mir, it seems (appears) to me
mir ist kalt, I am cold
mir ist bange, I am afraid
es tut mir leid, I am sorry
es geht mir gut, I am well, am getting on well
mir ist . . ., I feel . . .
mir ist nicht wohl, I do not feel well
es geschieht mir, it happens to me, I happen to
es gelingt mir, I manage to, succeed in
es fällt mir ein, it occurs to me
es nützt mir nichts, it is of no use to me
es gefällt mir, it pleases me, I like

The following are Impersonal as in English:

es folgt, it follows
es genügt, it suffices
es scheint, it appears
es schlägt, it is striking (*clock*)

Exercise 75

It appeared quite funny to me. I am glad that you
have arrived. It was snowing when we left Bonn.
There were several soldiers in the inn. Were there
any ships in the harbour? It was striking two o'clock
as we drove past the Town Hall. I am sorry, we have
no more English newspapers. Do you like it in Berlin?
She does not like her new car. How are you getting on?
Are there any stamps (die Briefmarke, *singular*) in the

drawer? Did she manage to pass her examination? [1] How many people (die Person, *sing.*) are there in the compartment? There are no slaves (der Sklave) in this country. It bores me to stay here. So it appeared to me. I have succeeded [2] in learning this difficult language (die Sprache). Please shut [3] the window, I am cold. He is sorry he cannot come this evening. I felt as though I had not washed for (seit) weeks. That is no concern of yours. Is there a draught?

A NOTE ON OVERGROWN ADJECTIVES

There is one construction, of which the Germans are very fond, that causes a good deal of difficulty in actual translation. It consists in using a iong clause, including a Past Participle, as an adjective before a noun. The clause is preceded by an article or a demonstrative, and the Past Participle is declined as an adjective. No exercises on this construction are given in this book, as it is a difficult one to use in turning English into German; but as the construction frequently occurs in German you had better study carefully the following examples.

We might say in English, *an old man richly dressed*. In German this would run, *an old richly-dressed man* = ein alter, reich gekleideter Mann.

So the sentence, *I saw the wood that he sold to the steamers stopping there*, becomes ich sah das Holz, das er an die dort anlegenden Dampfer verkaufte.

> Die beiden, unmittelbar zusammenliegenden und nur durch eine schmale Veranda getrennten Blockhütten bestanden auch nur je aus einem Zimmer. The two immediately-lying-together-and-only-by-a-small-veranda-separated log-huts consisted (were made up) indeed only of a single room (each).

---

[1] *I pass an examination*, ich bestehe eine Prüfung.
[2] Gelingen is conjugated with sein.
[3] *To shut* is more usually zu-machen, and *to open*, auf-machen.

Here all the words joined together by hyphens really make up one overgrown adjective qualifying Blockhütten.

> Jetzt hob sich langsam ihr dunkles, in Tränen schwimmendes Auge zu dem seinen. Now her dark,-in-tears-swimming eye rose slowly to his.

In plain English this might be, *she slowly raised her dark eyes full of tears to his.*

> Ich rette Dich von der Dir verhassten Verbindung. I rescue thee from the to-thee-hateful engagement.

In ordinary English we would use a verb to complete the sense: *the engagement which is hateful to thee.*

Sometimes this qualifying clause runs to great length and includes subordinate clauses within itself:

> Der alte Hermann, ein tüchtiger Arbeiter, gab sich mit dem kleinen, aber trefflich rentierenden Geschäft vollauf zufrieden, und war mit den, allen alten ihm teuren Mustern und Formen völlig widersprechenden Zeichnungen des Malers Holaus, welche ihm eines Tages sein Sohn brachte, durchaus nicht einverstanden.

> Old Hermann, a capital workman, was quite content with the little-but-exceedingly-profitable business, and was not at all in sympathy with the (to-all-the-old,-to-him-dear-patterns-and-fashions-completely-opposed) drawings of the painter Holaus, which his son brought to him one day.

In the above, all between the parentheses is really one adjective qualifying *drawings*, though widersprechenden is the only word that " agrees with " Zeichnungen. In English we might split up this enormous adjective like this: *the drawings which were completely opposed to all the old patterns and fashions which were dear to him.*

When in translation you come across a passage that seems to make nonsense, you will very often find that one of these sentence-adjectives is the cause. By seeing how much of the sentence you can hyphen together as an adjective you will in most cases bring out the true meaning.

PART II

KEY TO EXERCISES

Exercise 1

The brother is poor. The father is not bad. Is the uncle here? No, he is there. Is the shop not here? Yes, it is here. The baker is often quite dishonest. The pupil is sometimes angry. Is the apple not good? No, it is bad. Is the garden beautiful? Yes, it is beautiful. Is the teacher always friendly? No, he is sometimes angry. Is the uncle poor? No, he is quite rich.

Exercise 2

Die Brüder sind arm. Die Väter sind nicht schlecht. Sind die Onkel hier? Nein, sie sind dort. Sind die Läden nicht hier? Ja, sie sind hier. Die Bäcker sind oft ganz unehrlich. Die Schüler sind manchmal böse. Sind die Äpfel nicht gut? Nein, sie sind schlecht. Sind die Gärten schön? Ja, sie sind schön. Sind die Lehrer immer freundlich? Nein, sie sind manchmal böse. Sind die Onkel arm? Nein, sie sind ganz reich.

Exercise 3

The city is very old. Is the nut ripe? The cow is not brown. The maid is not very tall. Is the night not dark? Is the sausage ready? The wall is very beautiful. Is the hand brown? No, it is white. Is the cow thirsty? No, it is hungry. The city is not old, it is new. Is the mouse always small? The maid is sometimes very friendly. The nut is old and sour. The night is quite black. The maid is tall and thin.

Exercise 4

Die Städte sind sehr alt. Sind die Nüsse reif? Die Kühe sind nicht braun. Die Mägde sind nicht sehr gross. Sind die Nächte nicht dunkel? Sind die Würste fertig? Die Wände sind sehr schön. Sind die Hände braun? Nein, sie sind weiss. Sind die Kühe durstig? Nein, sie sind hungrig. Die Städte sind nicht alt, sie sind neu. Sind die Mäuse immer klein? Die Mägde sind manchmal sehr freundlich. Die Nüsse sind alt und sauer. Die Nächte sind ganz schwarz. Die Mägde sind gross und dünn.

Exercise 5

The song is not very beautiful. The wheel is round. Is the village not small and very old? The egg is not round. The roof is red. The book is not too heavy. Is the glass not empty? No, it is almost too full. Is the word easy? No, it is very long and difficult. Is the child big? No, it is very small. The house is fairly tall. Is the field round or square? It is square. The dress is quite new but it is not very beautiful. The leaf is long and green. Is the house not too low?

Exercise 6

Die Lieder sind nicht sehr schön. Die Räder sind rund. Sind die Dörfer nicht klein und sehr alt? Die Eier sind nicht rund. Die Dächer sind rot. Die Bücher sind nicht zu schwer. Sind die Gläser nicht leer? Nein, sie sind fast zu voll. Sind die Wörter leicht? Nein, sie sind sehr lang und schwer. Sind die Kinder gross? Nein, sie sind sehr klein. Die Häuser sind ziemlich hoch. Sind die Felder rund oder viereckig? Sie sind viereckig. Die Kleider sind ganz neu, aber sie sind nicht sehr schön. Die Blätter sind lang und grün. Sind die Häuser nicht zu niedrig?

Revision Exercise

Sind die Gärten lang und schön? Sie sind schön, aber sie sind nicht sehr lang. Ist der Schneider immer ehrlich? Ja, er ist immer ehrlich. Ist das Glas immer voll? Nein, es ist oft leer. Sind die Städte alt oder neu? Sie sind alt. Die Felder sind fast immer grün. Sind die Nüsse nicht reif? Die Äpfel sind zu grün und sauer. Ist das Haus gross oder klein? Es ist sehr gross. Sind die Läden immer leer? Nein, sie sind selten leer. Sind die Mägde gross und dünn? Nein, sie sind klein und dick. Sind die Kinder immer gut? Nein, sie sind manchmal sehr böse. Die Nacht ist lang und sehr dunkel. Der Bruder ist arm, aber ganz ehrlich, und der Vater ist reich, aber ganz unehrlich. Die Lieder sind zu lang und zu schwer. Hier ist das Dorf und dort (or da) ist das Haus. Das Kind ist fast immer hungrig.

Exercise 7

Wir besuchen. Ihr sucht. Sie sagen. Telefonieren sie? Die Brüder lachen. Die Mägde kochen. Spielen die Schüler? Ihr sagt. Wir hören. Sie hassen. Sie suchen.

Exercise 8

Träume ich? Du antwortest. Er zeichnet. Der Onkel reist. Das Kind atmet. Hören Sie? Sie arbeitet. Der Bruder hasst. Ich lächle. Antwortet der Lehrer?

Exercise 9

(a) Ich höre die Kuh. Der Onkel hasst die Magd. Die Mägde kochen die Würste. Wir lieben die Magd. Du suchst die Nüsse. Die Schneider machen die Kleider. Der Bruder besucht das Dorf. Ich reiche die Gläser. Die Kinder hassen das Lied. Sie zeichnet das Haus. Ich lächle, aber sie weint.

(b) Wir suchen die Kühe. Ich höre die Mäuse. Schicken Sie die Bücher? Raucht sie? Tanzen Sie

nicht? Arbeitet der Vater? Spielen die Kinder?
Kocht die Magd die Blätter? Träume ich? Weinst
du? Atmet das Kind?

Exercise 10

Do you visit (are you visiting) the uncle? I look (am
looking) for the eggs. The brother visits (is visiting)
the shop. The tailor passes (is passing) the dress.
The teacher looks (is looking) for the pupil. We hear
the schoolboys (pupils). The baker sends (is sending)
the sausages. The maid cooks (is cooking) the apple.
She cooks (is cooking) apples.

Exercise 11

Hören Sie das Lied? Ich besuche den Bruder. Wir
suchen den Lehrer. Der Schüler sucht Eier. Ich
zeichne das Haus. Der Lehrer sagt das Wort. Der
Vater besucht den Onkel. Sie antwortet nicht. Besucht
der Onkel die Stadt? Du besuchst den Bäcker.

Exercise 12

The uncle passes the nuts to the father. The maid
sends the apples to the brother. The father answers the
tailor. The baker sends nuts and apples to the teacher.
You pass the apple to the father. We send books and
clothes to the maid. I pass the egg to the child.

Exercise 13

Der Lehrer schickt dem Vater das Buch. Die Magd
reicht dem Onkel die Nüsse. Die Schüler reichen dem
Lehrer die Bücher. Wir schicken der Magd Eier und
Äpfel. Der Schüler antwortet dem Vater. Die Magd
reicht dem Schneider das Kleid. Ich reiche dem Bäcker
das Glas. Sie antworten dem Lehrer.

Exercise 14

The baker's shop is beautiful and new. The uncle's
cows are big and brown. The wheels of the carriage

(*or* cart) are round. The maid's dress is red. The walls of the house are white. The houses of the villages are small. The child's glass is empty. The teacher opens the pupils' books. The tailor's brother sends the dress to the father's maid. Do you not hear the children's songs? I telephone to the baker's father. The tailor's maid sends apples and nuts to the baker's brother. The cow's horns are not very long. The maid's hands are small and white, but the brothers' hands are quite big and red.

Exercise 15

Die Hörner der Kühe sind nicht zu lang. Ich telefoniere dem Bruder der Magd. Das Dach des Hauses ist viereckig und rot. Der Vater des Schülers antwortet dem Lehrer. Die Magd des Onkels schickt dem Bruder des Schneiders Eier und Äpfel. Besucht er nicht den Schneider des Dorfes? Hören Sie nicht das Lied der Magd? Die Läden der Bäcker sind ganz voll. Der Bruder des Bäckers hört die Lieder der Kinder. Ich schicke dem Schneider das Kleid der Magd nicht.

Exercise 16

We are Frenchmen. Where do the brothers of the sailor live? They do not live here. Did you tell the sailors' song to the boy? Are the Frenchman's nephews upstairs? No, they are downstairs. Are the boy's hares living (alive)? No, they are dead. The boys drew the lions. Did you not learn the sailor's song? We did not often visit the Frenchman's nephew. The horns of the ox are very long. They sent apples, nuts and eggs to the sailors.

Exercise 17

Wo wohnen Sie? Lebt der Hase noch? Nein, er ist tot. Schickten Sie dem Neffen des Bäckers das Buch des Jungen (des Knaben)? Wo ist das Haus des Matrosen? Es ist dort. Wo sind die Ochsen des Franzosen?

Sie sind nicht hier. Ist das Haus der Franzosen nicht weiss? Nein, es ist rot; dort ist das Dach des Hauses. Lernt der Neffe des Matrosen das Lied nicht? Rauchte der Neffe des Franzosen? Nein, er rauchte nicht, er arbeitete. Spielen die Kinder des Matrosen? Ich lachte, aber sie weinte. Wohnten Sie oben oder unten?

Exercise 18

Wir sind arm, aber Sie sind reich. Marie ist oben und Peter spielt unten. Gretchen und Paula haben den Hasen. Er ist gross und braun. Hat der Matrose den Ochsen? Bist du noch dort? Ja, ich bin hier. Haben die Matrosen Gläser? Ja, sie haben Gläser, aber sie sind leer. Wo sind wir? Wir sind oben. Wo spielen die Neffen des Matrosen? Sie sind dort. Hast du Kühe und Ochsen? Nein, aber ich habe den Hasen.

Exercise 19

The nuts and apples were not ripe. The teacher's nephew was upstairs. The maid's brothers were dead. The uncle's cows were big and brown. I had the hare, but it is dead. Was the pupil's father very angry? No, he was fairly friendly. Was the sailor's glass empty? No, it was quite full. Had you the garden? Yes, it was very beautiful. Where were you? I was upstairs.

Exercise 20

Wo war der Matrose? Er war nicht hier. Waren die Lehrer dort? Ja, und (auch) die Schüler. War der Lehrer immer freundlich? Nein, er war oft sehr böse. Hatten Sie das Haus dort? Ja, wir hatten das Haus und den Garten. Waren die Würste fertig? Nein, aber wir hatten Äpfel und Nüsse. Ich war sehr durstig und das Glas war ganz leer.

Exercise 21

Which child is playing in the garden? This child is playing in the garden with the tailor's nephew. Were there ten cows in that field? No, there were eight oxen there. Each schoolboy had four books. In which class are you? I am in this class. Were you very poor after the war? The baker sent the nephew out of the room. In which village did you live? We lived in this village in that house there.

Exercise 22

Hatte jedes Kind fünf oder sechs Äpfel? Welcher Lehrer schickte dem Vater dieses Buch? Die drei Kinder waren in der Kirche. Ich schickte die Kinder zu der (or zur) Schule. Waren acht oder neun Häuser in jenem Dorf(e)? Es waren sieben. Es sind fünf Lehrer in dieser Schule, und es sind zehn Kinder in jeder Klasse. In welchem Haus(e) wohnen Sie? Welches Lied lernten Sie? Welchen Jungen schickten Sie aus der Klasse? Welche Kuh hörten Sie? Er schickte neun Eier mit dem Kleid(e). Jedes Kind in jenem Dorf hat drei oder vier Bücher. In welchem Zimmer ist der Neffe des Matrosen? Er ist oben im (in dem) Zimmer des Onkels.

Exercise 23

der Mantel	1	des Mantels	die Mäntel
das Fenster	1	des Fensters	die Fenster
die Tür	4	der Tür	die Türen
der Stock	2	des Stock(e)s	die Stöcke
die Socke	4	der Socke	die Socken
der Hut	2	des Hut(e)s	die Hüte
die Mütze	4	der Mütze	die Mützen
der Anzug	2	des Anzugs	die Anzüge
der Knopf	2	des Knopfes	die Knöpfe
der Strumpf	2	des Strumpfes	die Strümpfe
die Uhr	4	der Uhr	die Uhren
die Taschenuhr (as for Uhr).			
der Handschuh	2	des Handschuhes	die Handschuhe
das Haar	2	des Haar(e)s	die Haare
das Bein	2	des Bein(e)s	die Beine
das Licht	3	des Licht(e)s	die Lichter
der Tag	2	des Tag(e)s	die Tage
der Vogel	1	des Vogels	die Vögel
die Brust	2	der Brust	die Brüste
der Kragen	1	des Kragens	die Kragen

Exercise 24

The ambassador from Berlin is now in London. I sent my brother to Geneva. There are no apples in the garden. Our house is in this street. A Spaniard from Madrid is downstairs. Have you my gloves? He is the nephew of a teacher in Cologne. Where is your watch? Here it is. Otto's suit was in this room. Is this your hat? Where is Marie? Is this not your wrist-watch? Their maid's nephew is dead. I pass (hand) my uncle his hat. Our cows are in the field. Marie Smith's uncle is in Paris, and William's father is in Switzerland. Fritz's sister is in her uncle's shop.

Exercise 25

Schickte er keine Strümpfe mit den Schuhen? Ihre Kleider sind immer sehr gut. Ich schicke oft meinen Neffen in Deutschland Äpfel und Nüsse von (or aus) meinem Garten. Wir besuchen manchmal unseren Onkel in der Schweiz. Schickten Sie Ihren Neffen nach Genf oder nach Rom? Die Schuhe von Max sind schwarz und Giselas Handschuhe sind braun. Wo ist das Haus Ihres Onkels? Es ist in London. Sind die Zimmer seines Hauses sehr gross? Er schickte keine Knöpfe mit ihren Kleidern. Haben Sie eine Pariser Zeitung? Mein Onkel hat kein Auto. Schickten Sie die Bücher meines Bruders nach London? Die Häuser unserer Stadt sind gross und schön.

Exercise 26

die Fürstin	die Blume
die Eiche	das Kindlein
der Honig	die Treppe
das Leben	der Regen
die Eselei	der Edelstein
der Teppich	die Fröhlichkeit
der Februar	das Büchlein
das Gold	die Melodie
die Übersetzung	das Eisen
die Schlacht	der Löwe

der Garten
(das) Griechenland
die Stunde
der Jüngling
die Reinheit
(das) Paris
die Freundschaft
der Diamant
die Schrift
die Poesie
das Rauchen
der Freitag
die Frau

die Sonne
der Liebling
das Väterchen
die Dummheit
(das) Helgoland
der Käfig
das Tanzen
der Monat
das Pferdchen
der Kuchen
die Union
das Blümchen

Exercise 27

Have you sent the teacher's book to the baker's nephew? I have heard the lions in the wood. Has the maid not cooked (boiled) the apples? My brother has telephoned to my father. I have handed my uncle his stick. This girl has played the piano. Do you like smoking cigarettes? No, I always smoke a pipe. At Christmas we send our brother apples, nuts, books and cigarettes. Do you like listening to music on the wireless? We have lived in a house in that village. The soldiers have burnt the capital of the country. My sister has looked for the advertisement in the (news)-paper. We have called our dog Mops. Which book has your sister chosen? The soldiers have killed no women and children. In the summer we have often bathed in the sea. The pupils have played with the snow in the winter. I do not like dogs.

Exercise 28

Hast du geträumt? Nein, ich habe jenes Haus gezeichnet. Welches Buch ist auf Ihrem Stuhl? Dieser Teppich ist sehr alt. Ich höre gern Radio. Raucht Ihr Vater gern? Ja, er hat immer Zigarren geraucht. Ich rauche oft Zigarren zu Weihnachten. Im Sommer haben wir unseren Onkel in der Schweiz besucht. Haben Sie jene Zeitungen nach Genf geschickt? Der Bäcker und seine Frau haben ihr Kind Margarete genannt. Der Schneider hat das Kleid nicht gemacht. Ottos Schwester hat Klavier gespielt, und meine Brüder haben die Musik an dem (or am) Radio gehört. Hat der Schneider das Kleid gebracht? In welchem Laden haben Sie jenen Hut gekauft? Baden Sie gern in der See? Ich höre gern das Grammophon.

Exercise 29

I have heard nothing (I have not heard anything). Yesterday the sun was quite warm. To whom did you send the Christmas-tree? I have sent it to my nephew. Those clouds are big and black, they bring rain. The weather is very cold and there is fog (mist) on the river. When did you buy this suit? I bought it yesterday in that shop. Was it cheap or dear? It was quite cheap. The stars are small, but the moon is big. Have you sent the wrist-watch to your sister? Yes, I sent it to her yesterday. Has your father sent the Christmas-tree to the children? Yes, he sent it to them yesterday. There are three dogs on the lawn; my nephew is playing with them.

Exercise 30

Die Sonne war gestern nicht sehr hell. Wann haben Sie geantwortet? Es waren sieben oder acht Matrosen auf dem Fluss. Dieser Fluss ist sehr lang. Wir hörten kaum das Lied der Kinder. Wen haben Sie in der Schweiz besucht? Diese Autos sind fast zu billig. Wem haben Sie gestern telefoniert? Hier ist Ihr Hut. Wo haben Sie ihn gekauft? Ich schicke ihn meinem Bruder. Die Kinder haben die Äpfel gesucht. Ich habe sie ihnen gereicht. Wir haben nie(mals) Nebel in diesem Lande. Wer hat ihm geantwortet? Haben Sie ihr telefoniert? War der Wind gestern sehr stark? Der Himmel war blau und die Wolken waren klein und weiss. Das

Wasser in dem Teich war gestern zu kalt. Wir haben nicht gebadet. Ich habe ihm nichts gesagt. Sie lächelte nur. Wir hörten sie kaum.

Exercise 31

The spider was big and fat; it spun a web. The bee hummed (buzzed); it flew from flower to flower and looked for honey. What does the wasp eat? It eats sugar. The donkeys brayed (were braying), the pigs grunted (were grunting), the dogs barked (were barking) and the cats mewed (were mewing). The farm-hand rode a horse. He fed the oxen, the sheep and the cows. His dog was running with him. He barked too loudly. The farmer struck him with his whip. The farmer's wife milked the cows in the stable. There are eight or nine farm-hands on the farm. They are always working. In the autumn they plough the fields. In the spring they sow. The farmer's name was Mr. Brown. He got up and began his work. He drove in his cart to the field. What did he eat? He ate bread and drank tea with sugar. His children sang songs. He gave them apples and nuts.

Exercise 32

Der Bauer fuhr zu den Feldern. Er nahm seine Kinder. Sie sahen gern die Kühe, Schafe und Pferde auf den Feldern. Der Junge hiess Karl. Er ritt gern auf einem Esel. Er gab ihm Heu. Der Esel frisst gern Zucker.

Karls Hund ist in dem Garten. Er ist gross und stark. Er bricht die Blumen. Karl läuft nach ihm und schlägt ihn mit seiner Peitsche. Der Hund bellt laut. Die Sonne ist warm und hell. Die Bienen summen und fliegen von Blume zu Blume. Sie fressen gern Honig. Essen Sie gern Honig? Karl sieht die Spinne nicht. Sie ist gross und dick. Sie hat ein Gewebe gesponnen. Haben Sie gern Spinnen?

Haben Sie Ihre Arbeit schon begonnen? Ich habe

meine Uhr zerbrochen. Hat Ihr Onkel seinem Neffen eine Uhr gegeben? Hast du deinen Tee getrunken? Ja, und ich habe mein Brot und meinen Honig schon gegessen.

Exercise 33

Our bank lies between the post-office and St. Mary's Church. I telephoned to my brother from a call-box. There are many skyscrapers in our city. The building of the League of Nations was in Geneva, in Switzerland. There were Bolsheviks in Russia and Fascists in Italy and Germany. The soldiers are at (before) the gate of the city. They are Italians and Spaniards.

I went into the restaurant. I had a meal (= ate) and paid (for it). I came out of the restaurant and went to the market-place. I went into the cinema. The cinema was big and beautiful, but it was not a skyscraper. In the cinema there were men, women and children. I often go to the theatre. Do you like going to the theatre? I saw a hospital near the park. Opposite the big stores was the Town Hall. This building is magnificent. I said to a policeman: " Where is there a letter-box? " He replied: " There at the street-corner." I put a letter in the letter-box. My brother is employed at a grocer's. He sells sugar, tea, etc. Behind the Town Hall was St. Paul's Church. I went under a bridge. This bridge was very high. Over the bridge travel cars and horses. The traffic is very dangerous for pedestrians.

Exercise 34

Ich legte mein Buch auf einen Stuhl. Das Wetter war ziemlich warm. Ich lief aus dem Zimmer. Ich ging durch die Tür und auf die Strasse. Es war dunkel, aber die Strasse war wegen der Strassenlampen ganz hell. Es waren acht Autos und drei Pferde auf der Strasse. Ich ging mit meinem Hund um die Stadt. Mein Hund lief zwischen die Autos. Ich ging in eine Telefonzelle und telefonierte meiner Schwester. Sie ist in einem Krankenhaus neben der Paulskirche angestellt. Ich wohne mit meinem Bruder gegenüber dem Rathaus. Wir gingen nach rechts und kamen zu einer Brücke. Sie war ziemlich niedrig. Wir sahen auf den Verkehr. Der Verkehr ist seit dem Krieg(e) sehr gefährlich. Mein Onkel war in jenem Auto. Er fuhr zum (zu dem) Markt-platz. Er hat einen Laden dort. Er fährt oft über diese Brücke. Unser Dorf lag jenseit(s) des Flusses. Vor unserem Hause stand eine Strassenlampe. Wir gingen in ein Restaurant, um zu essen. (Wir gingen zum Essen in ein Restaurant.) Nach dem Essen ging ich nach Hause ohne meinen Hund, aber ich sah ihn zu Hause, vor der Tür.

Exercise 35

To-morrow I shall go to the market-place. What will you do there? I shall buy two or three horses. Are they cheap or dear? They are fairly dear this year. Will you go by car? To-day the weather is very cold. We shall soon have (be having) snow. What will your uncle do (be doing) next Tuesday? He will fly (go by air) to Lisbon. This afternoon we shall go to the cinema. Do you like going to the cinema? My brothers will fly to Cologne one day. This evening my sister will play the piano and Else's brother will sing songs. I shall listen to the music on the wireless. I like the wireless (I like listening to the wireless).

Yesterday I had a letter from my uncle. At Christmas he will send my father a Christmas-tree. He was in France last week. The weather was very cold there. They have been having fog and rain. I have never been to France. Have you ever been to Paris?

Exercise 36

Nächsten Freitag werde ich nach Deutschland fahren. Werden Sie mit dem Auto nach London fahren? Nein, ich werde mit der U-Bahn (Untergrundbahn) fahren. Was werden Sie in Deutschland tun? Ich werde einen oder zwei Freunde besuchen. Werden Sie mit dem Flugzeug fahren? Nein, ich fahre nicht gern mit dem Flugzeug. Waren Sie schon in Deutschland? Ja, ich war letztes Jahr dort. Zu welchem Bahnhof werden Sie gehen? Nach Liverpool Street. Das Wetter ist nicht sehr warm gewesen.

Exercise 37

ein grosser Baum	eines grossen Baumes	grosse Bäume
eine kleine Blume	einer kleinen Blume	kleine Blumen
kein blinder Mann	keines blinden Mannes	keine blinden Männer
ein kleines Mädchen	eines kleinen Mädchens	kleine Mädchen
welche breite Strasse	welcher breiten Strasse	welche breiten Strassen
der starke Hund	des starken Hundes	die starken Hunde
die kluge Kusine	der klugen Kusine	die klugen Kusinen
der taube Vetter	des tauben Vetters	die tauben Vettern (see p. 189. 6)
die hässliche alte Frau	der hässlichen alten Frau	die hässlichen alten Frauen
kalter Wind	kalten Windes	kalte Winde
derselbe schmutzige Junge	desselben schmutzigen Jungen	dieselben schmutzigen Jungen

Exercise 38

The sad girl is always weeping. German books are not always difficult. The fat baker's little daughter gave a letter to the old tailor's clever nephew. A clever boy learns quickly. The little children played on the soft grass. They do not like playing on the hard street. The old grandfather is blind, and his old wife is very deaf. The pretty girl is wearing a new dress with red buttons. Charles has a clean handkerchief in the pocket of his brown suit. The traffic in these narrow streets is very dangerous. Two blind men went (were going) with their white dog across the broad (wide) street. Pretty girls are not always silly.

Exercise 39

Kleine Jungen (Knaben) sind fast immer schmutzig. Ich werde einen alten Freund in Genf besuchen. Blinde Männer sind nicht immer traurig. Die engen Strassen der alten Stadt waren sehr dunkel. Ich habe diesen unbequemen alten Stuhl nicht gern. Meine schöne Kusine sang französische, spanische und deutsche Lieder. Ich höre sehr gern gute Musik am Radio. Der italienische Gesandte kam gestern nach London. Maries Kusine trug ein grünes Kleid und einen weissen Hut. Welches deutsche Buch haben Sie gewählt?

Exercise 40

The man to whom I spoke yesterday is the Mayor of Brussels. A great film-actress plays a part in the film which we shall see this evening. The landlord of the " Red Lion " Inn, in which (where) I met the chauffeur of the film-actor Willi Fritsch yesterday, has been a sailor. The cobbler who mended your brown shoes is at the door. The butcher served (was serving) his customers, amongst whom was the maid of a great author. The basket in which she was carrying the apples and nuts was quite new. The dentist in whose house the policeman arrested the thief pulled out (extracted) my tooth this morning. The typist who took down this letter is dead.

Exercise 41

1. Der Briefträger, dessen Schwester unser Kindermädchen ist, hat einen Brief gebracht. 2. Der Mann, mit dem ich gesprochen habe, ist der Neffe eines grossen Richters. 3. Die Schublade, in der (worin) ich den Brief sah, war fast leer. 4. Die Frau, deren Mann wir gestern in der " Blauen Kuh " sahen, ist sehr reich. 5. Der Kellner bediente den Jäger, der bei einem sehr reichen Kaufmann angestellt ist. 6. Der Dieb, der die

F

Armbanduhr einer grossen Filmschauspielerin stahl, ist
der Bruder eines Polizisten. 7. Das Kino, in dem ich
diesen Film sah, war gross und prachtvoll. 8. Der
Arzt, der meinen Neffen geheilt hat, ist nach Ägypten
gegangen. 9. Die Brüder, deren Flugzeug verunglückte,
sind im Krankenhaus.

Exercise 42

Die beiden (Die zwei) Mädchen, deren Vater eine
grosse Rolle im Film " Michael Kohlhaas " spielte, hörten
Radio. Der Brief, den ich in dieser Schublade sah, war
von Ihrem Bruder. Das Kindermädchen, das die
Kinder spazieren geführt hat, ist aus Köln. Der Arzt,
dessen Neffen ich gestern traf, heilte meine Schwester in
der Schweiz. Das Haus, in dem er wohnte, hatte ein
rotes Dach und eine grüne Tür. Die Stenotypistin, die
diesen Brief nach Diktat schrieb, hat einen Bruder, der
bei Ihrem Onkel angestellt ist. Der Mann, mit dem ich
gestern sprach, ist der Wirt des " Lustigen Bauers."
Das Café, in dem wir ihn trafen, ist neben dem Postamt
(neben der Post). Alles, was wir sahen, war weiss.
Der Briefträger hat einen Brief, der von Russland
kommt. Am Bahnhof sahen wir die Brüder, die letztes
Jahr nach Amerika flogen. Der Kellner, dessen Brüder
das Auto der Schauspielerin stahlen, bediente den Schutzmann, der sie verhaftete. Nichts, was er tut, ist sehr
gut. Das Wetter war hell und warm, was unsere Arbeit
leicht machte.

Exercise 43

1. Dann wohnte ein armer Fischer in diesem Dorfe.
2. Bald trafen wir die Sekretärin des Schriftstellers am
Bahnhof. 3. Dann bauten die Russen neue Schulen
und Universitäten. 4. Plötzlich lief der Hund aus dem
Zimmer. 5. Eines Tages kam der Schneider nach
Hause.

Exercise 44

1. Er ging ins Hospital, weil er krank war. 2. Da ich nicht dort war, kam er nach Hause. 3. Ich werde den Brief schreiben, sobald (wenn) ich nach Hause komme. 4. Ich werde meinen Freund besuchen, bevor ich ins Kino gehe. 5. Er trägt keinen Mantel, obgleich es sehr kalt ist. 6. Da wir eine Erkältung hatten, gingen wir ins Bett. 7. Obgleich er sehr reich war, war er sehr traurig. 8. Das Mädchen ging ins Bett, da sie sehr müde war. 9. Wenn ich sie traf, lächelte sie immer. 10. Als ich die Schublade öffnete, sah ich die Taschenuhr.

Exercise 45

Es regnete, als der Fischer über den See ruderte. Er fing keine Fische, da die Fische nicht hungrig waren. Meine Kinder hörten die Lieder der deutschen Kinder am Radio, während ich diese Aufgabe schrieb. Sobald er nach Hause kommt, wird er Ihnen telefonieren. Schlossen Sie nicht die Türen (machten Sie nicht die Türen zu), bevor Sie ins Bett gingen? Wenn ich nach Berlin fahre, werde ich Ihren Onkel besuchen. Da sie nicht zu Hause waren, steckten wir den Brief in den Briefkasten. Es schneite, als wir zum Bahnhof fuhren. Er spricht Deutsch, Französisch, Englisch und Italienisch, obgleich er nie (mals) in diesen Ländern gewesen ist. Sie arbeiteten, bis es ganz dunkel war. Als das (Dienst)mädchen an die Tür kam, bat der Mann um Brot und Tee. Wir fuhren mit dem Boot über den See, obschon es ganz dunkel war.

Exercise 46

The thief did not answer me. Did you not meet her at the station? Who gave you this beautiful book? There are many cherries and apples in the garden. Yes, I have already seen them. I shall give some to my friend. My little sister asked me for sweets. I gave her some, but she has already eaten them. " Another

glass, please," I said to the waiter, but he did not hear
me. At Christmas Uncle Fritz will pay us a visit. We
still have some butter in the pantry. Do you like rolls
with butter and cheese? We have no more oranges. Do
you drink coffee with or without cream? With cream,
if you have any. Both brothers were there. Have you
no other bananas? I have some more, but they are not
ripe. I shall buy you an ice, if you pick me some peas
and beans in the garden. Have you any more tea in the
pot? Is anybody at the door? I see nobody there (I
do not see anybody there). They have heard everything
you told me yesterday. Everyone in the village has his
long garden, in which he has potatoes, beans, peas,
apples, cherries, etc. People drink a lot of coffee in
Germany. I had no plate, but the waiter has brought
me one.

Exercise 47

Man trinkt mehr Tee in England. Haben Sie (etwas)
Kaffee im Speiseschrank? Ja, ich habe ein wenig.
Wenn Sie nicht genug Bücher haben, habe ich noch eines
hier. Unser Onkel gab uns einige Bonbons und Apfelsinen. Ich esse gern Apfelsinen. Der Jäger trank noch
ein Glas Wein. Es sind noch einige Kartoffeln im
Garten, wenn Sie nicht genug hier haben. Die spani-
schen Mädchen pflückten Apfelsinen und Zitronen und
sie gaben uns einige (davon = of them). Haben Sie
Milch oder Sahne? Das Frühstück in der "Blauen
Kuh" war ziemlich billig, aber das Mittagessen im
"Roten Löwen" war sehr teuer, und man gab uns
keinen Kaffee. Ich esse Käse nicht gern. Ist noch
etwas Zucker in der (Zucker)dose? Der Kellner hat
mir ein anderes Messer gebracht, da dieses schmutzig
ist. Zum Abendessen werden wir Kirschen und Bananen
mit Sahne haben. Der Kellner wird Ihnen noch etwas
Suppe bringen. Jedermann war schläfrig, aber niemand
ging ins (zu) Bett. All(e) seine Freunde sind in Amerika.

Einige Schafe waren auf dem Feld. Er spricht ein (sehr) wenig Deutsch, aber kein Spanisch. Wer hat all(e) die Kirschen gegessen?

Exercise 48

The father said to the children: " Do you want to go for a run in the car this evening to Berlin? " " Oh, yes, rather! " cried the children. They had to wear their new clothes (suits), because they were to visit their (girl and boy) cousins in Berlin. They could not (were not able to) leave the house before three o'clock, because their mother was not ready. " Can I go to Berlin by bicycle (on my bike)? " asked young Charles. " Oh, no," answered the father. " It is much too slow by bicycle. You must come with us."

Soon they were all ready. The father can drive very well. " I must buy some more petrol," he said, " the (petrol-)tank is nearly empty." So they stopped at a petrol-station. Then they came to a cross-roads. The red light was showing and they had to wait. Mr. Smith's car can climb well and they travelled rapidly on the way to Berlin. At half-past three they were in Berlin. There they saw a poor motor-cyclist who was repairing a burst tyre. On (in) the wide streets of Berlin they saw 'buses, trams, cars, taxis and bicycles. There the traffic is very dangerous. They went up a one-way street, so they had to go backwards. Above the city they saw a large aeroplane which was to fly to America. Many pedestrians were hurrying across the street and it was (a) good (thing) that the horn (hooter) was in order. But they could always (were always able to) go pretty (fairly) quickly and overtook (passed) many other cars. Then the car stopped and Mr. Smith beckoned to a policeman. He had to ask the way. Soon, however, they were before the (their) uncle's house.

Exercise 49

Sie können nach Berlin fahren (or gehen), wenn Sie wollen. Ich soll heute abend den Zahnarzt besuchen. Darf ich hier rauchen? Ich will meinen Hund im Park spazieren führen. Er sollte gestern nach Paris fliegen, wurde aber plötzlich krank. Wir mussten zu Fuss nach Hause gehen. Da er kein Deutsch sprechen konnte, nahm er mich mit. Sie sollen gleich zu Bett gehen. Hier spricht man Deutsch. Soll ich (etwas) Brot kaufen? Sie sollen mit niemand sprechen. Wir konnten wegen des Nebels das Flugzeug nicht sehen. Dürfen wir (können wir) heute abend ins Kino gehen? Wir mussten mit der Taxe fahren. Wenn das Wetter warm ist, können Sie heute nachmittag im See baden. Wir wollen Ihre Kühe und Schafe sehen. Ich kann es Ihnen nicht sagen. Da mein Bruder Sie nicht besuchen kann, schickt er Ihnen einen Brief.

Exercise 50

Tragen Sie diesen Brief auf die Post. Gehen wir um die Stadt spazieren. Ich habe nach Berlin fahren müssen. Sie hat Spanisch lernen müssen. Sie haben Ihr Buch nicht finden können. Er soll morgen London verlassen. Hast du diesen Film sehen können? Er wollte nicht antworten. Meine Schwestern mussten mit dem Flugzeug fahren. Ich kann kein Schwedisch (sprechen). Kann sie Holländisch? (sprechen: in such expressions the infinitive sprechen is often omitted). Wir haben Ihnen nicht viele Äpfel schicken können, da der Sommer zu schlecht gewesen ist. Wir konnten wegen des Nebels nicht sehr schnell fahren. Sie können (if you can is impersonal: man kann) zum Bahnhof mit dem Autobus fahren. Wollen Sie uns ein Lied singen? Ich kann nicht singen, da ich eine böse Erkältung habe.

Exercise 51

Waiter, bring us two glasses of beer, please. Taxi, drive quickly to the station! Give me an ice, please. Let us go to the cinema. Please weigh this letter for me. Please pass me the sugar. Let us go to the theatre this evening. Open the door, please. Ask the policeman the way. Let us go to London to-morrow. Please tell me where I can find a taxi. Buy me some (a few) cigarettes. Give me a London (news)paper.

Exercise 52

The Millers wanted to go to Cologne. They looked for a fast train (an express) in the time-table. Their luggage was quite ready. They went by taxi to the station. Mr. Miller bought the tickets at the booking--office. They had to hurry to platform nine. The porter carried the luggage. Hilda bought some sweets and Mrs. Miller chose a few newspapers from the bookstall. As the train was late they waited for a bit in the waiting-room. Then the train came in. The porter put the luggage in the luggage van and Mr. Miller gave him a tip. They all entered an empty compartment. Hilda and Max chose the corner seats, as they wanted to look out of the window. Mr. Miller put his attaché case on the rack.

The engine whistled and they then set off (then off they went). As they were in a smoking compartment Mr. Miller began to smoke. He likes (smoking) cigarettes. In Aix-la-Chapelle they had to change. At half-past twelve they went along the corridor to the dining-car. After lunch they returned to their compartment. Max had to go to the lavatory, because his hands were frightfully dirty. Mr. Miller yawned. He was tired and he began to sleep. When they arrived punctually in Cologne they alighted quickly. At the station they saw Uncle Otto and Aunt Gisela. A porter fetched their luggage from the luggage-van. Mr. Miller gave up the tickets and they left the station. They travelled (went) up a long, narrow street and came to the house of their (= the) Uncle. They entered the house. They were all tired and hungry.

Exercise 53

Geben Sie mir drei Hinfahrtskarten nach Stettin, bitte! Lehnen Sie nicht zum Fenster hinaus! Träger, tragen Sie, bitte, mein Gepäck zum Schnellzug nach Köln! Chauffeur, fahren Sie schnell zum Bahnhof, sonst werde ich den Zug nach Koblenz versäumen. Muss ich in Aachen umsteigen? Ich verliess das Haus um halb sieben. Alle Plätze waren besetzt. Wir fuhren letzten Montag nach Berlin zurück. Ist ein Platz frei für mich? Der Durchgangszug fährt um halb zehn ab. Tante Marie holte sie vom Bahnhof ab. Haben Sie die Verbindung in Kassel versäumt? Ein grosser Herr trat in das Zimmer herein und sprach zu mir. Mein Hut ist in dem Speisewagen. Wenn Sie mit diesem Schnellzug fahren, werden Sie einen Zuschlag bezahlen müssen. Stellen Sie Ihren Koffer hin! Wohin fahren Sie? Wo haben Sie Ihre Handschuhe hingelegt? Wo sind die Fahrkarten?

Exercise 54

(a) Zweimal drei ist sechs.

Viermal fünf ist zwanzig.

Fünfmal sechs ist dreissig.

Siebenmal drei ist einundzwanzig.

Elfmal elf ist einhunderteinundzwanzig.

Siebenundzwanzig geteilt durch drei ist neun.

Einundachtzig geteilt durch neun ist neun.

Vierundvierzig geteilt durch vier ist elf.

Fünf und drei ist acht.

Neun und sechs ist fünfzehn.

Neunzehn und siebzehn ist sechsunddreissig.

Dreizehn und vierzehn ist siebenundzwanzig.

Dreiundvierzig und achtunddreissig ist einundachtzig.

Achtundneunzig weniger siebenundfünfzig ist einundvierzig.

Einhundertneununddreissig weniger siebenundachtzig ist zweiundfünfzig.

Eintausendsiebenhundertundsechzehn weniger siebenhunderteinundvierzig ist neunhundertfünfundsiebzig.

Einhunderteinundzwanzig geteilt durch elf ist elf.

Zweihundertundfünfzig geteilt durch fünfzig ist fünf.

Dreitausendneunhunderteinundzwanzig weniger eintausendneunhundertvierundsechzig ist eintausendneunhundertsiebenundfünfzig. Eintausendachthundertachtundachtzig weniger siebenhundertsiebenundsiebzig ist eintausendeinhundertundelf.

(b) Um neun Uhr—halb sieben—zwölf Uhr—vierzig Minuten nach eins (zwanzig Minuten vor zwei);

„ Viertel vor drei;

„ zwanzig Minuten nach drei;

„ zehn Minuten nach zwölf;

„ Viertel vor elf;

„ zehn Minuten nach elf;

„ zehn Minuten vor vier;

„ ein Uhr (um eins);

„ halb sechs;

„ Viertel vor sechs;

„ Viertel nach sieben;

„ zwanzig Minuten nach eins;

„ Viertel nach acht.

(c) Ein Drittel; zwei Fünftel; vier Neuntel; ein halb; drei Viertel; fünf Achtel; sechs Fünfundzwanzigstel.

erste, zweite, sechste, achte, sieb(en)te, elfte, zwölfte, achtzehnte, vierundzwanzigste, siebzehnte, dreissigste, neunundzwanzigste, hundertste, tausendste.

Exercise 55

London ist nicht so gross wie die Vereinigten Staaten. Die Erde ist kleiner als die Sonne. Die Themse ist nicht so lang wie der Rhein. Paris ist nicht so alt wie Rom. Das Gold ist nicht so hart wie das Eisen. Die Stadt ist grösser als das Dorf. Die Luft ist nicht so schwer wie das Wasser. Der Elefant ist stärker als der Mann. Die Katze ist falscher als der Hund. Der Knabe ist klüger als (nicht so klug wie, ebenso klug wie) das Mädchen. Der Schmetterling ist nicht so schnell wie die Schwalbe. Die See ist tiefer als der See. Der Eiffelturm ist höher als der Kölner Dom.

Exercise 56

How much do these apples cost?   Are these cherries
dearer than those (there)?   These are dearest.   Marie
is the nicest girl in the village.   Ottilie sings beautifully,
Hilda sings more beautifully, but Else sings most beautifully.   Which boy is the cleverest?   Otto is the cleverest,
but Konrad is almost as clever.   Is Belgium not as big
as Holland?   This girl is as pretty as her sister.   The
older a man gets, the less he can learn.   A higher (taller)
tree than that (one) is in our garden.   Can you speak
German?   Yes?   So much the better.   The sooner we
arrive the longer we shall have to wait.   The more he
drank the thirstier he became.   These bicycles are the
best.   Otto is the tallest boy in the class.   It is pleasanter
here in the garden than in the house.   Irmgard is more
diligent than her brother.   We must travel more carefully through this fog.   These cherries are the sweetest.
The garden looks prettier in the summer than in the
winter.

Exercise 57

Je fleissiger er arbeitet, desto weniger lernt er.   Das
Wasser ist heute kälter als gestern.   Es wird dunkler.
Es wurde langsam heller.   Otto ist gross, Konrad ist
grösser, und Wilhelm ist der grösste.   Marie singt süsser
als ihre Schwester.   Sind Sie (eben)so faul wie Ihr
Bruder?   Dieser Junge sieht nicht so klug aus wie sein
Bruder.   Je länger wir hier warten, desto dunkler wird
es sein, wenn wir nach Hause zurückgehen.   Ich habe
sehr wenig, sie hat weniger und ihre Kusine hat am
wenigsten.   Dieser Hund ist der treueste.   Ist jenes
Messer schärfer als dieses?   Ich antwortete aufs beste.
Ich werde die grössten und süssesten Äpfel kaufen.   Der
Lehrer wird dem klügsten Jungen dieses Buch geben.

Exercise 58

These gloves are mine, those are yours.   Do you
always read the same paper?   My house is not so big

as yours. Their (your, her) garden is longer than ours.
I have read my book and my brother's. I have seen
his car, but not theirs (hers). Those who come (too)
late must wait here. We always eat at the same restaurant. He has always lived in the same street. He who
does not work shall not eat. She has found my hat,
but not his.

Exercise 59

Das sind Ihre Bücher, nicht meine. Sein Bruder ist
klüger als der ihrige. Mein Messer ist schärfer als das
deinige. Beide Tanten wohnen in derselben Stadt. Er
liest dasselbe Buch. Die, die (Diejenigen, welche) nicht
fleissig arbeiten, werden nichts lernen. Ihre Bäume
sind höher als die unsrigen. Sie kauft immer dieselben
Bonbons. Unsere Stadt ist grösser als die Ihrige.
Seine Arbeit ist besser als die seiner Schwester. Sein
Haus ist nicht so klein wie das seines Onkels. Die, die
(Diejenigen, welche) am besten arbeiten, können früh
nach Hause gehen.

Exercise 60

Last summer we spent our summer-holidays on the
North coast of Germany. We packed our trunks (cases)
and set out on the 28th August for Swinemünde. The
weather was magnificent during the whole month which
we spent there. We stayed (lived) in a large hotel
which was near the beach.

Every (each) morning we got up early. After breakfast we went down to the beach. We took (carried)
our bathing-suits with us and when the weather was
warm we put on our bathing-costumes and caps and
swam in the sea. I cannot swim like a fish, yet I like
swimming. Some little children, whose parents were
sitting in deck-chairs, were making sand-castles. Others
played football or looked for shrimps and crabs with
their nets. After bathing we lay on the warm sand and
took a sun-bath. Soon we became quite brown, almost

like black men. One day we saw a boy in the sea. He
could not swim very well. A fisherman saved him from
drowning.

Sometimes we went for an outing in a fishing-smack.
That was very nice and we had a lot of fun (we enjoyed
ourselves). We dived from the boat into the sea. It
was quite nice when the waves were big. We often
climbed up the cliffs, or went for a walk along the beach.

My father had hired a beach-hut and so we could
have coffee in the afternoon on the beach. My father
often played golf on the beautiful golf-links. We were
quite sad when we had to return home.

Exercise 61

Ich will morgen früh nach Stuttgart abfahren. Im
Herbst müssen wir die Äpfel pflücken und die Felder
pflügen. Wo ist der Korb, in den ich die Äpfel legte?
Zu Weihnachten haben wir vier Tage Ferien. Wir
dürfen hier nicht rauchen, denn es ist verboten. Das
Kind, dessen Eltern tot sind, ist sehr klug. Ich kann
diesen Brief nicht lesen, weil er so schlecht geschrieben
ist. Darum müssen Sie mir den Brief zeigen, den Sie
heute morgen geschrieben haben. Gestern regnete es,
als ich die Strasse herauf kam. Der Mann, mit dem ich
gestern sprach, ist der Bürgermeister. Bevor Sie aus-
gehen, zeigen Sie mir die Zeitung, die Sie heute morgen
gekauft haben. Er ging gestern abend aus, obgleich
(obschon) er krank war. Da es so spät war, ging er
gleich (sogleich, sofort) zu Bett. Während er seinen
Mantel anzog, hörte er jemand an der Tür.

Exercise 62

Dieser Briefkasten wird dreimal am Tage vom Briefträger geleert. Dieser Brief wurde gestern von meiner
Stenotypistin geschrieben. Ist der Brief schon geschrieben? Ich werde meinen Freund in Bonn besuchen. Das
Telegramm wurde gestern geschickt. Als wir ankamen,

war die Tür schon geschlossen. Das Haus ist schon gebaut worden. Dieses Kleid wurde letztes Jahr vom Schneider gemacht.

Exercise 63

Ich bin von meinem Bruder gebeten worden, nach Berlin zu fahren. Diese Äpfel wurden gestern von den Kindern des Bäckers gepflückt. Wann werden diese Briefe geschrieben werden? Das Kind ist bestraft worden. Diese Zeitung wird jeden Tag von Tausenden von Männern und Frauen gelesen. Ist das Auto schon repariert worden? Sind Sie von jemand gesehen worden? Der Briefkasten wird jetzt vom Briefträger geleert. Dieses Kleid wird vom Schneider gemacht werden. Wann wurde dieses Buch geschrieben?

Exercise 64

I thanked him for his letter. He died of gout. He was annoyed at my answer. I asked for the price of the apples. He has translated this book from the German, while he was staying with his aunt. He ordered the man to wait for the train. The girl blushed at this answer. I entrust this work to you. To whom does the house with the red roof belong? Allow me to help you. I read the letter out to my mother. Describe to me the city in which (where) you live. Do you remember the day (when) we met the man? What has become of your brother? The boy (lad) leant against the wall. Follow me, please. Do you like it here in England? I do not like the English weather. You can rely on him. When did you give this wrist-watch to your sister? The others laughed and made fun of the poor boy. The little girl was afraid of the big cow. The poor man asked me for money. We trembled with cold.

Exercise 65

Die Mädchen und Jungen (colloquially: Mädels und Jungens) tanzten vor Freude. Mein Neffe ist Seemann

geworden. Ich erstaunte über seinen Brief. An wen
denken Sie? Fragen Sie nach dem Preis des Mantels
im Schaufenster! Reichen Sie bitte Ihrem Bruder den
Zucker. Gefiel Ihnen der Film gestern abend? Ich
glaube (es) ihr nicht. Haben Sie nicht nach dem Arzt
geschickt? Ich fürchte, dass wir morgen schlechtes
Wetter bekommen werden. Ich erlaubte den Kindern,
in dem Garten zu spielen. Wir erzählten dem Schutzmann die ganze Geschichte. Er bat mich um Geld,
aber ich schlug es ihm ab. Ich erinnere mich nicht des
Mädchens. Er regte sich über meine Antwort auf und
befahl mir, ihm das Buch zu zeigen. Er lehnte sich an
die Tür und wollte mir nicht erlauben auszugehen.
Fürchten Sie sich vor Löwen? Dort ist der Mann, dem
wir in dem " Roten Löwen " begegnet sind.

Exercise 66

Before going to bed he wrote a letter. After reading
the paper he went out. Putting on his coat and hat
he ran out of the room. Bathing is forbidden here.
He sat in the garden smoking a pipe. Who is the girl
wearing the green hat? We heard our cousin singing.
He remained standing at (or by) the door. Knowing
he was at home I telephoned him. On looking out of
the window I saw our doctor's car go by. He saw them
(or her) playing tennis. He smoked while shaving.
The little girl came running and spoke to us. I stood up
on seeing the man enter, but my sister remained sitting.

Exercise 67

Als ich den Brief auf dem Tisch sah, las ich ihn.
" Sind Sie fertig? " fragte er, indem er seinen Mantel
anzog. Er stand bei (or neben) der Tür und las eine
Zeitung. Der Mann arbeitete, und seine Frau spielte
Klavier. Ich bat ihn sich zu setzen, aber er blieb
stehen. Als wir die Schublade öffneten, fanden wir

einen Brief von ihm. Wer ist der Mann, der auf dem grossen schwarzen Pferd reitet? Wir fanden sie weinend. Bevor er ausging, telefonierte er seinem Bruder. Da wir wussten, dass es spät war, beschlossen wir, unseren Onkel nicht zu besuchen. Nachdem er die Anzeige in der Zeitung gesehen hatte, telefonierte er seiner Schwester. Der sterbende Matrose bat um Wasser. Der Mann stirbt. Als ich die Strasse entlang ging, begegnete ich meinem Zahnarzt. Ich kannte diesen Arzt. Er weiss nichts.

Exercise 68

I am going swimming this afternoon with my friend. Have you promised to send him a book? My uncle taught me to play the piano. I am getting (I get) my hair cut. I have had a new house built. Where did you learn to play golf? Help me to get in (i.e. *a vehicle*). Must you go home now? We shall have some new clothes made (for us) in Paris. He decided to go by car to Dresden. I decided to have my hair cut. My father has promised to meet me at the station. Do you wish to leave (set out) to-morrow? I ordered the waiter to bring me a bottle of wine. I have had a bottle of wine brought (for me). We saw him riding in the wood. Wash his hands! Have you washed your hands? I have washed his hands. The barber has cut the man's hair. Please do not cut my hair too short. Have you tinted your finger-nails and plucked your eyebrows? I have my shoes cleaned. Has he gone home? They have not yet arrived. My brother flew to Amsterdam yesterday.

Exercise 69

Ich hörte Sie im Garten singen. Wer hat Sie Klavier spielen gelehrt? Soll ich Ihnen einige Zigaretten kaufen, wenn ich in der Stadt bin? Wir sind zum Bahnhof geeilt, um Sie abzuholen. Sind Sie in Russland gereist?

Die Bäume in Ihrem Garten sind sehr hoch gewachsen.
Ich liess gestern das Gras des Rasens schneiden. Ich
werde nächste Woche einen neuen Anzug machen lassen.
Wir sind oft über diese Felder gewandert (or gezogen).
Sind Sie den ganzen Tag zu Hause geblieben? Können
Sie mir dieses Rad reparieren lassen? Ich habe Ihnen
ein Glas Wein bringen lassen. Soll ich Ihnen diese Sa-
chen zuschicken lassen? Ich habe beschlossen, mir die
Haare ondulieren zu lassen. Wollen Sie mich tauchen
lehren? Wir versprachen, ihnen jede Woche einen Brief
zu schicken. Er bat sie, ihm zu schreiben. Haben Sie
dem Kellner befohlen, noch etwas Brot zu bringen?
Nein, ich habe einige Zigaretten bestellt. Wollen Sie
Radio hören?

Exercise 70

Taxi, drive to an up-do-date but cheap hotel. I want
to spend a few weeks in this town. Here is a good
hotel, Sir, the " Riesenfürstenhof." Good! I'll get
out here. How much do I owe you? Three marks
fifty? Here is a tip for you. Thank you, Sir! That's
all right (Not at all, Don't mention it)! Can I have
(or get) a room for a few nights? Yes, certainly! What
sort of one? I do not want to spend too much.

The man said he had a few nice rooms which were quite
quiet and well lighted. I replied that I should like to
see them. He said I could go up by lift: Number 15.
I asked where the lift was. He replied that it was in the
corner. I asked the lift-boy if (or whether) the hotel
had central heating. " Yes, of course! " he answered.
He asked to what room I was going. I said I should
spend a few days there. I asked if (or whether) the
hotel had a garage. Whether the hotel had electric
light (= was lighted by electricity) in all rooms. He
replied that there was a bathroom near my room and
that there was central heating in all rooms.

I rang for the porter. I asked him if (or whether)

he would wake me up at 5 o'clock. He replied that he would not forget. I pulled up the blind and looked down upon the street.

Exercise 71

Der Chauffeur sagte, dass er ganz fertig sei (*or* wäre) (*or*: sagte, er sei (wäre) ganz fertig). Ich fragte ihn, ob er wüsste, wo das Hotel Bismarck sei (*or* wäre). Er sagte, dass er es nie(mals) gesehen hätte. Ich fragte den Schutzmann, ob die Post (das Postamt) in jener Strasse wäre (*or* sei). Sie sagte, dass er Montag käme (*or* kommen würde). Das Mädchen sagte, dass sie sein Auto in der Garage gesehen hätte. Der Mann sagte mir, dass sie nach England mit dem Flugzeug gefahren wäre (*or* sei). Ich antwortete, dass ich den Zug versäumt hätte. Sie fragte mich, ob ich mit ihnen spielen möchte. Es leben unsere Freunde aus Deutschland!

Exercise 72

Wenn Sie das Geld hätten, möchten Sie nach den Vereinigten Staaten (fahren)? Wenn ich Sie wäre, würde ich gleich nach Hause gehen. Wäre mein Freund zu Hause gewesen, dann hätte ich bei ihm übernachtet (hätte ich die Nacht bei ihm verbracht). Sie hätte den Zug versäumt (Si würde den Zug versäumt haben), wenn sie nicht mit der Taxe zum Bahnhof gefahren wäre. Ich hätte Ihnen telefoniert (Ich würde Ihnen telefoniert haben), wenn ich nicht hätte kommen können. Ich sagte ihnen, dass ich ihnen helfen würde, wenn ich könnte. Ich wäre sehr gern mit Ihnen ins Theater gegangen (Ich würde sehr gern mit Ihnen ins Theater gegangen sein), aber ich war furchtbar beschäftigt. Wenn der Aufzug (Fahrstuhl, Lift) in Ordnung gewesen wäre, so (*or* dann) wäre ich nicht die Treppe hinuntergefallen (so würde ich nicht die Treppe hinuntergefallen sein). Ich fragte ihn, wieviel ich ihm schuldig wäre (*or* sei). Er fragte mich, ob ich dort ausstiege (aussteige). Ich

fragte ihn, ob er das Licht anknipsen könnte. Er fragte
mich, ob ich mit dem Fahrstuhl hinauffahren wollte
(*or* wolle). Ich sagte ihm, dass ich jede Woche einen
Brief von ihr bekäme (bekomme). Der Chauffeur fragte
mich, zu was für einem Hotel ich gehen möchte (*or*
wollte). Ich sagte ihm, dass ich die Treppe herauf-
gekommen wäre (*or* sei). Der Liftjunge sagte, dass er
einen Wecker auf den Kamin in meinem Zimmer (*or*
meines Zimmers) gesetzt hätte (*or* habe). Das Mädchen
sah aus, als ob sie (*or* es) mehrere Wochen an der See
verbracht hätte.

Exercise 73
A Sea-Voyage from Ostend to Dover

A great desire of mine [1] was at last to be fulfilled.
My parents promised that I might visit a friend in London. Quite apart from the reunion with him (meeting
him, seeing him again) (I had not seen him for a year), I
was especially looking forward to the sea-voyage. I had
always heard and read so much about the beauty of
the sea that I longed (thereafter) to be allowed to admire
this beauty with my own eyes. I was not disappointed.
The day of my departure dawned at last. The clerk of
the weather seemed to me to be quite friendly, and the sun
beamed (*or* shone) quite brightly from the dark-blue sky.
After a long railway journey from Wiesbaden I arrived
at 4 o'clock in Ostend. I hired a porter to take my cases
on to the ship. Together with all the other passengers
I passed a barrier, where my passport was carefully
examined. They asked me if I had any (= had not any)
dutiable goods. I replied in the negative. After I had
opened my cases I was allowed (to go) through (*or* by).
I went across the wooden gangway on to the big boat.
It was a Belgian boat. A few sailors with bronzed faces
and weather-beaten features were hurrying about on the
deck. I had a look round the ship. I soon became

[1] Ein Freund von mir, a friend *of mine*.

acquainted with a young Englishman who had already made this journey several times and was a bit more conversant with everything. He showed me where we could sit comfortably and be protected from the wind. A loud, deafening blast of the siren indicated that we were ready to leave. We went (sailed, steamed) out of the harbour into the open sea.

The coloured sails of the fishing-smacks looked very beautiful in the sunshine. The sea, slightly ruffled by a pleasing fresh wind, gave a picturesque impression. Ostend, with its beautiful beach and the big hotels, retreated further and further away.

We went past the buoys which tinkled and tossed about in the water. After three hours' journey we could see the white coast of England. An hour later the travellers conversed merrily with one another and looked for their cases, in order to get ready for going ashore. The boat entered Dover harbour. The sun was already slowly sinking in the west. In Dover the immigration officers examined our passports and the customs officers examined our cases. I entered a compartment of the through-train for London which stood waiting and made myself comfortable. I had a cup of English tea brought to me. Then I felt like a giant refreshed. Thank Heaven! I had not been seasick!

Exercise 74

Er wäscht sich im Badezimmer. Sie hat sich die Hände schon gewaschen. Haben Sie (etwas) Geld bei sich? Haben Sie den Reifen selbst repariert (ausgebessert)? Die Tür öffnete sich und ein grosser Herr trat herein. Sie kleidet sich an, glaube ich. Ich fühle mich ganz komisch. Zwei Jungen waren an die Tür gelehnt und plauderten miteinander. Sie wandte sich (drehte sich) schnell um. Das Rathaus war in der Friedrichstrasse. Kein Blatt regte sich. Sie setzten sich auf den

Stuhl. Haben Sie sich rasiert? Sie kleideten sich
schnell aus. Ich will mich in der Stadt umsehen. Sie
irren sich, wenn Sie glauben, dass ich ein Franzose bin.
Ich habe mich erkältet. Wir haben uns vorgenommen,
einige Freunde in Bonn zu besuchen. Wir verirrten uns
in dem Walde. Erinnern Sie sich des Namens von unserem Hotel (unseres Hotels would sound unpleasant
after des Namens). Ich freue mich, dass Sie angekommen sind. Das Kind legte sich auf das Bett und weinte.
Warum regen Sie sich so auf? Meine Schwestern sehen
sich die Schaufenster an. Waschen Sie sich! Waschen
Sie sich die Hände! Drehen Sie sich nicht um! Setzen
Sie sich, bitte! Ich habe mir vorgenommen, einige Tage
in Dresden zu verbringen.

Exercise 75

Es kam mir ganz komisch vor. Es freut mich, dass
Sie angekommen sind. Es schneite, als wir Bonn verliessen. Es waren mehrere Soldaten in dem Wirtshaus.
Waren (lagen) einige Schiffe in dem Hafen? Es schlug
zwei Uhr, als wir am Rathaus vorbeifuhren. Ich be-
dauere (= I regret; *or* es tut mir leid), wir haben keine
englischen Zeitungen übrig.[1] Gefällt es Ihnen in Berlin?
Ihr neues Auto gefällt ihr nicht. Wie geht es Ihnen?
Sind einige Briefmarken in der Schublade? Gelang es
ihr (Ist es ihr gelungen), ihre Prüfung zu bestehen? Wie-
viele Personen sind (befinden sich) in dem Abteil? Es
gibt keine Sklaven in diesem Lande. Es langweilt mich
hier zu bleiben. So kam es mir vor. Es ist mir gelungen, diese schwere Sprache zu lernen. Bitte, machen Sie
das Fenster zu, mir ist kalt. Es tut ihm leid, dass er
heute abend nicht kommen kann. Mir war, als ob ich
mich seit Wochen nicht gewaschen hätte. Das geht Sie
nicht an. Zieht es?

[1] Übrig, left over, remaining; mehr would mean here no
longer, never any more.

CONCLUSION

The student who has conscientiously worked out the exercises and has followed our advice in reading German is now in a position to advance on his own account. He should buy a good dictionary ; a good choice would be *The E.U.P. Concise German Dictionary.*

To obtain greater mastery of the language it is necessary to write and read as much as possible. The student who follows our advice and finds a correspondent in Germany will find he is making good progress if his German friend is conscientiously helping him with his grammar and construction. This service, to be permanent and beneficial, must, of course, be mutual. The student should endeavour to study and sympathize with the views and likes and dislikes of his correspondent. If an exchange of visits can result from such a correspondence, so much the better.

If the student resides in London he will find it quite easy to purchase German magazines and newspapers, while German short stories are becoming increasingly more accessible to the English student for a modest outlay. For this purpose let him send for catalogues of German readers to such publishers as G. Bell and Sons, Portugal Street, London; Geo. G. Harrap and Co., 182 High Holborn, London; Oxford University Press, 11 Warwick Square, E.C.4; Cambridge University Press, 200 Euston Road, N.W.1; and the University of London Press, 10 Warwick Lane, E.C.4. The student should choose at first the short easy readers, priced about a few shillings. These are modern stories, dealing for the most part with adventure, crime-detection and the like.

When half a dozen or so of the foregoing have been read the student can begin the study of some of the classics, such as Lessing, Schiller, Goethe, Hebbel, Grillparzer, Heinrich von Kleist, Freytag, Sudermann or Hauptmann in drama, or Theodor Storm, Grillparzer, Jean Paul Richter, Keller, Meyer, Heyse, Freytag, Eichendorff, Hauff or von Kleist in prose fiction. The student can find details of works by the above in the catalogues already referred to. If he is interested in poetry the best anthology to buy is the *Oxford Book of German Verse*, from the Oxford University Press.

An excellent and very cheap edition of the works of the German classics is that by Ph. Reclam, Jun., of Leipzig. These can be had, either new or second-hand, from Foyle's, of Charing Cross Road, and for a few shillings the student can acquire quite a number of the best works in the literature of Germany.

The important thing is to read as much as possible, looking up just those words and idioms necessary for an appreciation of the matter. A close attention to the meaning of every word is only going to kill the interest and bring discouragement or boredom. The vocabulary and " feeling for the language " (das Sprachgefühl) will then come unconsciously and pleasantly.

By the time the student has progressed thus far upon the road, he will be able to dispense with his guide and proceed alone on a wonderful voyage of discovery, delighting in every fresh vista that opens up before his eyes. And in this interesting, nay, exciting enterprise we wish him " Glückliche Reise! "

APPENDIX A

TABLE OF GERMAN DECLENSIONS

A bracketed *Umlaut* means that not all the nouns indicated take the *Umlaut* in the plural. This is best learnt by saying for the four declensions: "Sometimes—sometimes—always—never."

1.	Sing.	Plural
		(..)
Nom.	——	——
		(..)
Acc.	——	——
		(..)
Gen.	——s	——
		(..)
Dat.	——	——n

1. Masc. and neuter nouns in -el, -en, -er : for those taking the *Umlaut* see List 1 overleaf.

2. Neuter nouns in -chen and -lein.

3. Two feminines :
   die Mutter (..)
   die Tochter (..)

2.	Sing.	Plural
		(..)
Nom.	——	——e
		(..)
Acc.	——	——e
		(..)
Gen.	——(e)s	——e
		(..)
Dat.	——(e)	——en

1. Most masc. monosyllables, *some not* taking the *Umlaut* (see List 2 overleaf).

2. About 30 feminine monos., *all* taking the *Umlaut* (see List 3 overleaf).

3. Some neut. monos., *none* taking the *Umlaut*.

4. Nouns in -ich, -ig, -ling, -nis, -sal.

5. A few masc. and neut. nouns with 4th Decl. plural (see List 6 overleaf).

3.	Sing.	Plural
		..
Nom.	——	——er
		..
Acc.	——	——er
		..
Gen.	——(e)s	——er
		..
Dat.	——(e)	——ern

1. The neuter monos. in List 4.
2. A few masc. monos. (List 5).
3. Nouns in -tum.
4. Der Vormund.

4.	Sing.	Plural
Nom.	——	——(e)n
Acc.	——(e)n	——(e)n
Gen.	——(e)n	——(e)n
Dat.	——(e)n	——(e)n

1. *All* other feminines.

2. All masc. nouns in -e (exc. der Käse, in Decl. 2).

3. Foreign words, stressed on last syllable, as der Student'.

Notes

1. Feminine nouns take *no ending* in the singular.
2. As a rule monosyllables take the -es of the Gen. sing. in Declensions 2 and 3, and words of more than one syllable take -s.
3. Words ending in -s in Declension 2 and in -in in Declension 4 double the final consonant before the ending : Autobus—Autobusse; Königin—Königinnen.
4. Notice all Declensions have -n in the Dative plural.

SPECIAL LISTS OF NOUNS

1. Nouns of Declension 1 taking the *Umlaut* in the plural :

   Masculine :

   Acker, field
   Apfel, apple
   Boden, ground
   Bruder, brother
   Faden, thread
   Garten, garden
   Graben, ditch

   Hafen, harbour
   Hammer, hammer
   Kasten, box
   Laden, shop
   Mangel, lack
   Mantel, coat
   Nagel, nail

   Ofen, stove, oven
   Sattel, saddle
   Schnabel, beak
   Schwager, brother-in-law
   Vater, father
   Vogel, bird

   Neuter : das Kloster, monastery

2. Masculine nouns of Declension 2 *not* taking the *Umlaut* in the plural :

   Aal, eel
   Apparat, apparatus
   Arm, arm
   Docht, wick
   Dom, dome, cathedral
   Fasan, pheasant
   Grad, degree
   Huf, hoof
   Hund, dog

   Kran, crane
   Lachs, salmon
   Lauch, leek
   Monat, month
   Mond, moon
   Omnibus, omnibus
   Park, park
   Pfad, path
   Puls, pulse

   Punkt, point
   Salat, salad
   Salm, salmon
   Schal, scarf
   Schuh, shoe
   Star, starling
   Stoff, stuff
   Tag, day
   Thron, throne

3. Feminine monosyllables of Declension 2 (*all* taking *Umlaut* where possible) :

   Axt, axe
   Bank, bench
   Braut, bride
   Brust, breast
   Faust, fist
   Frucht, fruit
   Gans, goose

   Hand, hand
   Haut, skin
   Kraft, power
   Kuh, cow
   Macht, might
   Magd, maid

   Maus, mouse
   Nacht, night
   Nuss, nut
   Stadt, city
   Wand, wall
   Wurst, sausage

4. Neuter nouns of Declension 3 :

Amt, office	Gespenst, ghost	Licht, light
Bad, bath	Glas, glass	Lied, song
Blatt, leaf	Glied, member	Loch, hole
Buch, book	Grab, grave	Nest, nest
Dach, roof	Gras, grass	Rad, wheel
Denkmal, memorial	Haus, house	Schloss, castle
Dorf, village	Horn, horn	Schwert, sword
Ei, egg	Huhn, chicken	Tal, valley
Fach, subject	Kalb, calf	Tuch, cloth
Fass, barrel	Kind, child	Volk, people
Feld, field	Kleid, dress	Weib, woman
Geschlecht, sex	Lamm, lamb	Wort, word
Gesicht, face	Land, country	

5. Masculine monosyllables of Declension 3 :

Geist, spirit, ghost	Mann, man	Wald, wood
Gott, god	Rand, edge	Wurm, worm
Leib, body		

6. Nouns, 2nd Declension in sing., 4th Declension in plural :

Masculine :

Bauer, farmer	See, lake	Strahl, ray
Mast, mast	Staat, state	Vetter, cousin
Nachbar, neighbour		

Neuter :

Auge, eye	Hemd, shirt	Insekt, insect
Bett, bed	Herz (-ens, -en),	Interesse, interest
Ende, end	heart	Ohr, ear

APPENDIX B

ALPHABETICAL LIST OF STRONG AND IRREGULAR VERBS

N.B.—(a) Verbs with a prefix having the same forms as the simple verbs are omitted. (b) Verbs with a prefix are given when the verb is not used alone. (c) The 2nd and 3rd singular present indicative and the singular of the imperative are given only when these forms are different from the regular forms of the verb. (d) Verbs marked with an asterisk (*) are conjugated with sein, the others with haben. (e) Parts of the verb in thick type indicate an irregularity in their formation.

Present Infinitive	Present Indicative (2nd and 3rd pers. sing.)		Imper. (2nd pers. sing.)	Imperfect		Past Participle
				Indicative	Subjunct.	
backen, to bake	bäckst	bäckt	—	buk	büke	gebacken
befehlen, to command	befiehlst	befiehlt	befiehl	befahl	**beföhle**	befohlen
beginnen, to begin	—	—	—	begann	**begönne**	begonnen
beissen, to bite	—	—	—	biss	bisse	gebissen
bergen, to hide	birgst	birgt	birg	barg	bärge	geborgen
betrügen, to deceive	—	—	—	betrog	betröge	betrogen
biegen, to bend	—	—	—	bog	böge	gebogen
bieten, to offer	—	—	—	bot	böte	geboten
binden, to bind	—	—	—	band	bände	gebunden
bitten, to ask	—	—	—	bat	bäte	gebeten
blasen, to blow	bläst	bläst	—	blies	bliese	geblasen
*bleiben, to remain	—	—	—	blieb	bliebe	geblieben
braten, to roast	brätst	brät	—	briet	briete	gebraten
brechen, to break	brichst	bricht	brich	brach	bräche	gebrochen

	Pres. 2nd sg.	Pres. 3rd sg.	Imperative	Past	Subjunctive	Past participle
brennen, to burn	—	—	—	brannte	**brennte**	gebrannt
bringen, to bring	—	—	—	brachte	brächte	gebracht
denken, to think	—	—	—	dachte	dächte	gedacht
*dringen, to crowd, press forward	—	—	—	drang	dränge	gedrungen
empfangen, to receive	empfängst	empfängt	—	empfing	empfinge	empfangen
empfehlen, to recommend	empfiehlst	empfiehlt	empfiehl	empfahl	**empföhle**	empfohlen
essen, to eat	isst	isst	iss	ass	ässe	gegessen
*fahren, to go, drive	fährst	fährt	—	fuhr	führe	gefahren
*fallen, to fall	fällst	fällt	—	fiel	fiele	gefallen
fangen, to catch	fängst	fängt	—	fing	finge	gefangen
finden, to find	—	—	—	fand	fände	gefunden
*fliegen, to fly	—	—	—	flog	flöge	geflogen
*fliehen, to flee	—	—	—	floh	flöhe	geflohen
fliessen, to flow	—	—	—	floss	flösse	geflossen
fressen, to eat, devour	frisst	frisst	friss	frass	frässe	gefressen
frieren, to freeze	—	—	—	fror	fröre	gefroren
geben, to give	gibst	gibt	gib	gab	gäbe	gegeben
*gehen, to go	—	—	—	ging	ginge	gegangen
*gelingen, to succeed	—	—	—	gelang	gelänge	gelungen
*genesen, to get better	—	—	—	genas	genäse	genesen
geniessen, to enjoy	—	—	—	genoss	genösse	genossen
*geschehen, to happen	—	geschieht	—	geschah	geschähe	geschehen
gewinnen, to win	—	—	—	gewann	gewänne	gewonnen
giessen, to pour	—	—	—	goss	gösse	gegossen

Present Infinitive	Present Indicative (2nd and 3rd pers. sing.)		Imper. (2nd pers. sing.)	Imperfect Indicative	Imperfect Subjunct.	Past Participle
gleichen, to resemble	—	—	—	glich	gliche	geglichen
gleiten, to slip, glide	—	—	—	glitt	glitte	geglitten
graben, to dig	gräbst	gräbt	—	grub	grübe	gegraben
greifen, to seize	—	—	—	griff	griffe	gegriffen
halten, to hold	hältst	hält	—	hielt	hielte	gehalten
hangen, to hang	hängst	hängt	—	hing	hinge	gehangen
hauen, to hew	—	—	—	hieb	hiebe	gehauen
heben, to lift	—	—	—	hob	höbe	gehoben
heissen, to be called	—	—	—	hiess	hiesse	geheissen
helfen, to help	hilfst	hilft	hilf	half	**hülfe**(ä)	geholfen
kennen, to know (a person)	—	—	—	kannte	**kennte**	gekannt
*kriechen, to creep	—	—	—	kroch	kröche	gekrochen
**kommen, to come	—	—	—	kam	käme	gekommen
laden, to load	lädst (ladest)	lädt (ladet)	—	lud (ladete)	lüde	geladen
lassen, to let	lässt	lässt	—	liess	liesse	gelassen
*laufen, to run	läufst	läuft	—	lief	liefe	gelaufen
leiden, to suffer	—	—	—	litt	litte	gelitten
leihen, to lend	—	—	—	lieh	liehe	geliehen
lesen, to read	liest	liest	lies	las	läse	gelesen
liegen, to lie	—	—	—	lag	läge	gelegen
lügen, to tell a lie	—	—	—	log	löge	gelogen
nehmen, to take	nimmst	nimmt	nimm	nahm	nähme	genommen
nennen, to name	—	—	—	nannte	**nennte**	genannt
pfeifen, to whistle	—	—	—	pfiff	pfiffe	gepfiffen

raten, to advise	rätst	rät	—	riet	riete	geraten
reiben, to rub	—	—	—	rieb	riebe	gerieben
reissen, to tear	—	—	—	riss	risse	gerissen
*reiten, to ride	—	—	—	ritt	ritte	geritten
*rennen, to run	—	—	—	rannte	**rennte**	gerannt
riechen, to smell	—	—	—	roch	röche	gerochen
ringen, to struggle, wrestle	—	—	—	rang	ränge	gerungen
*rinnen, to flow	—	—	—	rann	ränne	geronnen
rufen, to call	—	—	—	rief	riefe	gerufen
scheinen, to shine	—	—	—	schien	schiene	geschienen
schieben, to shove	—	—	—	schob	schöbe	geschoben
schiessen, to shoot	—	—	—	schoss	schösse	geschossen
schlafen, to sleep	schläfst	schläft	—	schlief	schliefe	geschlafen
schlagen, to strike	schlägst	schlägt	—	schlug	schlüge	geschlagen
*schleichen, to creep	—	—	—	schlich	schliche	geschlichen
schliessen, to shut	—	—	—	schloss	schlösse	geschlossen
schneiden, to cut	—	—	—	schnitt	schnitte	geschnitten
schreiben, to write	—	—	—	schrieb	schriebe	geschrieben
schreien, to cry out	—	—	—	schrie	schriee	geschrieen
*schreiten, to step	—	—	—	schritt	schritte	geschritten
*schweigen, to be silent	—	—	—	schwieg	schwiege	geschwiegen
*schwimmen, to swim	—	—	—	**schwamm**	**schwömme**(ä)	geschwommen
*schwinden, to vanish	—	—	—	schwand	schwände	geschwunden
schwingen, to swing	—	—	—	schwang	schwänge	geschwungen
schwören, to swear	—	—	—	schwor (schwur)	schwüre	geschworen
sehen, to see	siehst	sieht	sieh	sah	sähe	gesehen

Present Infinitive	Present Indicative (2nd and 3rd pers. sing.)		Imper. (2nd pers. sing.)	Imperfect		Past Participle
				Indicative	Subjunct.	
*sein, to be	bist	ist	sei	war	wäre	gewesen
senden, to send	—	—	—	sandte	**sendete**	gesandt
singen, to sing	—	—	—	sang	sänge	gesungen
*sinken, to sink	—	—	—	sank	sänke	gesunken
sinnen, to think, ponder	—	—	—	sann	**sönne**	gesonnen
sitzen, to sit	—	—	—	sass	sässe	gesessen
sprechen, to speak	sprichst	spricht	sprich	sprach	spräche	gesprochen
*springen, to spring, jump	—	—	—	sprang	spränge	gesprungen
stehen, to stand	—	—	—	stand	stände	gestanden
stehlen, to steal	stiehlst	stiehlt	stiehl	stahl	**stöhle**(ä)	gestohlen
*steigen, to climb	—	—	—	stieg	stiege	gestiegen
*sterben, to die	stirbst	stirbt	stirb	starb	**stürbe**	gestorben
stossen, to push	stösst	stösst	—	stiess	stiesse	gestossen
streichen, to strike, spread	—	—	—	strich	striche	gestrichen
streiten, to struggle, quarrel	—	—	—	stritt	stritte	gestritten
tragen, to carry, wear	trägst	trägt	—	trug	trüge	getragen
treffen, to hit, meet	triffst	trifft	triff	traf	träfe	getroffen
treiben, to drive	—	—	—	trieb	triebe	getrieben
*treten, to step	trittst	tritt	tritt	trat	träte	getreten
trinken, to drink	—	—	—	trank	tränke	getrunken
tun, to do	tust	tut	—	tat	täte	getan
verderben, to spoil	verdirbst	verdirbt	verdirb	verdarb	**verdürbe**	verdorben
vergessen, to forget	vergisst	vergisst	vergiss	vergass	vergässe	vergessen

verlieren, to lose	—	—	—	verlor	verlöre	verloren
verzeihen, to pardon	—	—	—	verzieh	verziehe	verziehen
*wachsen, to grow	wächst	wächst	—	wuchs	wüchse	gewachsen
waschen, to wash	wäschst	wäscht	—	wusch	wüsche	gewaschen
weisen, to show	—	—	—	wies	wiese	gewiesen
wenden, to turn	—	—	—	wandte	**wendete**	gewandt
*werden, to become	wirst	wird	**werde**	wurde (ward)	würde	geworden
werfen, to throw	wirfst	wirft	wirf	warf	**würfe**	geworfen
wiegen, to weigh	—	—	—	wog	wöge	gewogen
wissen, to know (a fact)	weiss, weisst, weiss	weiss	wisse	wusste	wüsste	gewusst
ziehen, to draw, pull	—	—	—	zog	zöge	gezogen
zwingen, to force, compel	—	—	—	zwang	zwänge	gezwungen

ADVERTISING & PUBLICITY   ALGEBRA   AMATEUR ACTING
BOOK-KEEPING   BRICKWORK   BRINGING UP CHILDREN   BU
CHESS   CHINESE   COMMERCIAL ARITHMETIC   COMMERCIA
COMPOSE MUSIC   CONSTRUCTIONAL DETAILS   CONTRACT BRID
SPEEDWORDS   ECONOMIC GEOGRAPHY   ECONOMICS   EL
ENGLISH GRAMMAR   LITERARY APPRECIATION   ENGLISH REN
REVIVAL   VICTORIAN AGE   CONTEMPORARY LITERATURE   E
FREELANCE WRITING   FRENCH   FRENCH DICTIONARY   FREN
LIVING THINGS   GEOLOGY   GEOMETRY   GERMAN   GER
GOOD CONTROL OF INSECT PESTS   GOOD CONTROL OF PLANT
GOOD FARMING BY MACHINE   GOOD FARM WORKMANSHIP
GOOD MARKET GARDENING   GOOD MILK FARMING   GOOD PIG
GOOD ENGLISH   GREEK   GREGG SHORTHAND   GUIDEBOOK
GREAT BOLIVAR BOTHA   CATHERINE THE GREAT   CHATHAM
LIBERALISM   HENRY V   JOAN OF ARC   JOHN WYCLIFFE   LENIN   LC
ROBES   HAST
HOUS   EPA
WRITE   ND
MECH   **GIVE INSTRUCTION**   LCR
MOTO   FICI
PHYSI   **TO A WISE MAN···**   DE
ADMI   NG
PHR   OOK   SAILING   SALESMANSHIP   SECRETA   ACT
DEBATE   SPELLING   STAMP COLLECTING   STUDE   DE
TYPEWRITING   USE OF GEOGRAPHY   WAY TO POETR
COOKERY FOR GIRLS   DOGS AS PETS FOR BOYS AND GIRLS
PHOTOGRAPHY FOR BOYS AND GIRLS   RADIO FOR BOYS   RIDI
SOCCER FOR BOYS   STAMP COLLECTING FOR BOYS AND GIRLS
ACTING   ANATOMY   ARABIC   ASTRONOMY   BANKING
CHILDREN   BUSINESS ORGANISATION   CALCULUS   CANASTA
COMMERCIAL ART   COMMERCIAL CORRESPONDENCE   COMI
CONTRACT BRIDGE   COOKING   CRICKET   DRAWING   D
ECONOMICS   ELECTRICITY   ELECTRICITY IN THE HOUSE   EL
ENGLISH RENASCENCE   ENGLISH RENASCENCE TO THE ROMAI
LITERATURE   ETCHING   EVERYDAY FRENCH   TO EXPRESS YC
DICTIONARY   FRENCH PHRASE BOOK   GARDENING   GAS II
GERMAN   GERMAN DICTIONARY   GERMAN GRAMMAR   GER
CONTROL OF PLANT DISEASES   GOOD FARM ACCOUNTING
GOOD FARM WORKMANSHIP   GOOD FRUIT FARMING   GOOD
GOOD MILK FARMING   GOOD PIG KEEPING   GOOD POULTRY
GREGG SHORTHAND   GUIDEBOOK TO THE BIBLE   HINDUSTAN
CATHERINE THE GREAT   CHATHAM CLEMENCEAU CONSTANTINE
ARC JOHN WYCLIFFE   LENIN LOUIS XIV   MILTON PERICLES PETER
USE OF HISTORY   WARREN HASTINGS   WOODROW WILSON   HO
HOUSEHOLD ELECTRICITY   HOUSE REPAIRS   ITALIAN   JOIN
MANAGEMENT   MATHEMATICS   HAND TOOLS   ENGINEERI
DRAUGHTSMANSHIP   METEOROLOGY   MODELCRAFT   MODERN
MUSIC   NORWEGIAN   PERSONAL EFFICIENCY   PHILOSOPHY   O
SHORTHAND   PLANNING AND DESIGN   PLUMBING   POLISH